When Hearts Surrender

*Memories in a
Shoebox & Other
Keepsakes*

**Poetry by
Ronald Montgomery**

When Hearts Surrender
Shoebox & Other Keepsakes
All Rights Reserved.
Copyright © 2019 Ronald Montgomery
v2.0 r1.0

The opinions expressed in this manuscript are solely the opinions of the author and do not represent the opinions or thoughts of the publisher. The author has represented and warranted full ownership and/or legal right to publish all the materials in this book.

This book may not be reproduced, transmitted, or stored in whole or in part by any means, including graphic, electronic, or mechanical without the express written consent of the publisher except in the case of brief quotations embodied in critical articles and reviews.

Outskirts Press, Inc.
http://www.outskirtspress.com

ISBN: 978-1-9772-1323-5

Author Contact
SPIRIT2Spirit.Poetry@Yahoo.com

Outskirts Press and the "OP" logo are trademarks belonging to Outskirts Press, Inc.

PRINTED IN THE UNITED STATES OF AMERICA

Other books

by **Ronald Montgomery**

Tears of a Rose

Escape from Cape Coast Castle

Rare Flowers in Life's Garden

Only Love

Psalm of the Heart Fortress

No Turning Back

The Journey is Not Over

Transformation

Let's Heal STL

Spirit 2 Spirit

Cover & Chapter Graphic Designs
by Raeann Minella

Book Editors
Diane Ashburner
Linda C. Stewart

Consultant for Selected Works
Jayci L. Williams

Preface

In efforts to understand my life and my place here, I write. It is this effort that aids me in bringing into focus a kaleidoscope of experiences, expressions and stories that I've lived, or been influenced by. I have distilled them into the lines of my poems, and share them here with my children, friends and fellow life-travelers, in hopes that they will be of value.

These experiences have guided me to the belief that not everything in my life is within my power to control. I do believe that we are the co-creators of our experiences by way of the decisions we make and the actions we take. However, much of the framework in which I operate, is only mildly influenced by my hand. I have yet to be able to *make* someone else happy. And the seasons are adamant in refusing to be managed by me. I smile as I write this, because this conviction leads me to a place of peaceful acceptance. I now surrender to forces that I cannot change, and the seasons change absent my consent or consultation.

Clearly, this is no new wisdom, but putting the principle into operation on a daily basis is sometimes challenging for me. And when I am challenged, I write about my experiences, and about daily encounters with people and events that capture my attention.

I have met and continue meeting wonderful people who share their stories with me. Some have walked with me for a time to bless me with insights, shadings and colors for my word pictures, and then departed to continue their own journeys. I am thankful for these shared times. They are blessings and gifts of great value to me.

The poems in this volume are alive. They are the pictures, sketches, notes, and maps that trace past and present passages through seasons of my life and point the way to future discoveries. In some instances, my poems provide historical references. For others, they may be emotion-laden reminders of "buried" and untold stories.

Since I suspect and hope that some of my readers were born long after events I describe in my poems, I have also included "Reflections" that provide explanations of my references, allusions and metaphors.

If you are one of my frequent readers, you may notice that some poems have been changed from the originally published versions.

Some changes are stylistic. These point to the fact that my writing style has changed – much like my countenance.

Now a bit more wrinkled, compared to a once smooth me, I now re-pen more nuanced editions of decades-old thoughts that were simpler in the original versions, or maybe just different. I encourage you to be the judge of this.

But, since this is an anthology, I have attempted to share the best versions of current and earlier works. In some instances, I have changed words to provide better connections to today's cultural reference points. In other instances, I have added a "Reflection" to explain the relevance of words or situations.

I have experienced events directly or vicariously, and I add reflections for the sake of clarity and to give credit to the individual or circumstance that motivated me to write.

As I visit family and friends who have now reached a time in life, when dementia is assaulting their abilities to remember yesterday, or to look forward to tomorrow with anticipation, I recognize the greater importance of each memory. With this realization, I am hyper vigilant about capturing my memories. With time, the seasons of my life and the memories I have collected become even more valuable to me.

Despite this focus, I know that many memories are fading, while others persist and gain renewed vigor with each retelling. For me, these are like glowing embers in a smoldering campfire. They are eager to re-ignite an image or light the way as fuel of attention is added.

In some poems, my viewpoint has changed radically since the original writing. Now, several decades later, my 20/20 hindsight is aided by the bifocals of experience and "wisdom." With this "improved view," I feel compelled to make substantive modifications and provide improved versions here.

There is yet another aspect to my writing for which I will ask your indulgence.

Because my writing is genuinely guided by the desire to connect my readers with the experiences being referenced, I make comments in parentheses throughout the book. These are insights into my emotions or thoughts, that fall into my frame of reference or consciousness, at the times when I am creating or rewriting poems in this manuscript.

I call these insights my "emotional-reflectives." No, you won't find that in any dictionary. (I smile) Oops, there's one.

As I write and remember, or conversely remember and write, I sit at my PC and smile, frown or chuckle - wryly or merrily as the case may be. You would never know this unless I told you.

But, if I recounted the poem or story to you in person, you would know by my countenance that something was happening within me as part of the "spoken word delivery." Since you are not here, I will tell you what I am feeling and thinking. This is my attempt at sharing my authentic communication with you.

In my efforts to connect with readers, I have taken liberties with rules and laws of grammar and writing styles. This editorial license also includes liberties with the spelling of words, literal definitions, or inferred meaning. In most instances, I will point this out by bolding, italicizing or underlining.

For those who may be insulted or distracted by my liberty with the language and grammar, I apologize and request that you please "get over it." (I smile)

In virtually all instances, these liberties will be intentional. I assure you that my proofreaders have beaten me relentlessly and I have consciously resisted their urgings to press the backspace key or to follow rules. Poetry is about artful expression (artistic liberties). Right?

Now, after many reviews and edits, I am satisfied that I have given you my best efforts.

Because my writing and your reading are interactive and connected, I look forward to, and appreciate hearing your thoughts and reactions.

You may reach me at spirit2spirit.poetry@yahoo.com. Please indicate "Book Feedback" in the 'Subject' line to distinguish it from a host of other emails.

I thank you for buying this book as it allows me to live quietly and look out at the ocean (my vision several years ago, that is now reality) from my deck, as I write. (I smile.)

I hope you enjoy the poems shared here, and that they have value to you, as they do to me.

Acknowledgements

Many thanks go to understanding friends and family members who have helped me in my writing pursuits. Your critical eyes and probing questions have helped me to improve my writing skills and have added depth to my observations.

If I suddenly left a gathering or family meal, it might well have been because our conversations gave birth to a new idea, to some line, or to some inspiring word picture. Hopefully, I reached the birthing chamber – my computer, a napkin or the back of an envelope soon enough to capture a new creation before the inspiration faded.

I am especially thankful to those individuals who resisted the urge to run when I asked for them to proofread the manuscript, or to provide a review.

Because of this book's length, working with this volume has proven a bit more onerous than any of my previous efforts. Your edit suggestions have provided invaluable assistance to me in eliminating errors big and small, and in refining my delivery style and messages.

I would also like to acknowledge those who have contributed ideas that I have used as seeds in my "Inspiration Garden." Many of these were like mustard seeds that have now grown into trees. Others are dandelions that broke relentlessly through layers of concrete, to show small but beautiful faces in a sea of gray.

To fellow travelers who have contributed depth to my understanding by sharing heartfelt experiences and introspections, I say "Thank you… Thank you… I bless You."

I thank the "old souls" for sharing their best moments, and for repeating them lest I miss something. Thank You for allowing me to erase my missteps as I perfect telling the stories you've told me. Although I share them in my own words, I pray that the sentiments are equally as viable in the framework I provide, as the original telling.

I thank my sisters and friends who are the critical editors verifying that even loose grammar is the result of conscious decisions for the sake of creative expression. I thank you for your brilliance, loyalty and dedication even when I resisted change with such determination.

When asked about the greatest influencers for me in my lifetime, I am quick to admit that the greatest heroes in my life have been women. They are my sisters and friends, who have shepherded my steps and provide candid feedback and guidance.

To my God-Father, I am grateful for my view now. From my deck and office windows, I see the ever-present ocean waves breaking on the beach. They are testimony that faith has become the substance of my reality.

Thanks also to the many readers who have taken time to embrace the experiences captured in these pages. You have shared your thoughts, questions and feelings in feedback, and I appreciate it. You will find answers to many of your questions in the latter pages of this book.

I look forward to your continued feedback. I will attempt to respond to all messages at spirit2spirit.poetry@yahoo.com. Please reference the book's title and "feedback" in the subject line to get my immediate attention.

I look forward to sharing more of life's experiences with you in upcoming volumes. Again, thank you.

Table of Contents

PREFACE	II
ACKNOWLEDGEMENTS	V
DAWN – SEASON 1	2
SUNDAY MORNING WORSHIP	4
REFLECTION ON SUNDAY MORNING…	5
TEARS OF A ROSE…	5
FIRST LINES… IN THE DIARY OF "A RAINY DAY SISTER…"	5
SUNLIGHT PRISMS	6
AWESOME - A CELESTIAL SIGH…	6
FINDING FAITH	7
IN AWE	8
CRYSTAL KISSES…	9
A PERFECT PAIR	10
DOGMA	10
LIGHTING FIRE TO READY TINDER	11
REFLECTION ON "LIGHT FIRE TO READY TENDER"	12
A PERFECT PETAL…	13
HOPES' ARRIVAL…	14
HOLIDAYS…	14
REFLECTION ON "WAITING."	222
THE PATH TO PRAYER	15
WISDOM	15
FEAR REFRAMED	16
IN NEED OF NEW BEGINNINGS	17
LOVE'S RE-TREAT	18
NO LONGER A SECRET GARDEN…	18
CONTINUING DIARY… OF "A RAINY DAY SISTER…"	19
WATER LILIES OR LOVE NOTES	19
NO EDITS ON YESTERDAY	20

NOW AND THEN…	22
INCURABLE…	23
FRIENDS	23
REFLECTION ON FRIENDS	24
YOU SHINE…	25
ANTHEM	25
TO NIKKI	25
REFLECTION ON "TO NIKKI"	26
CASTING SEEDS TO THE AIRE…	26
A NEW DAY DAWNING…	27
WHO WAS SHE?	27
"EVASIVE…"	28
RUBY	29
A FINISH LINE REVIEW	30
NEXT PEACE	31
FLIGHT LESSONS – SEASON 2	32
MY BEDSIDE GARDEN…	34
A WAKE-UP…	34
REFLECTION ON "SHORT-TIMER"	35
J' ADORE	36
IF POEMS…MUSE-ICAL	36
SIMPLE UNDERSTANDING	37
SUNSET CELEBRATION	37
HEART CAPES	38
ALMOST A WOMAN…	39
ROUGH SPOTS	40
J. B. SIMPLE(LY) ENLIGHTENED	41
SMITTEN	42
FAMILY…	43
HE	44
PARADISE COME FULL CIRCLE	45
MY WAY HOME – SEASON 3	46

FREEDOM'S DANCE	48
SWEET DREAMS...	49
WORKING OUT	49
BROKEN	50
CONCENTRATED TRUTH JUICE...	51
REFLECTION ON TRUTH JUICE	52
MY PLANS IN HIS TIME...NEW NORMAL	53
DON'T WANNA BE NO ACCIDENT...	53
THE REVOLUTIONARY'S MANIFESTO	54
DARK NIGHT OF THE SOUL...	55
LIBERATION DAY	56
EXHAUSTIBLE	57
MY LOVE WON'T WAIT...	58
"PICTURE PERFECT" ...	59
IN THE TWINKLE OF AN EYE...	60
(BLACKENED) ROSE...	61
ONE DEGREE OF SEPARATION...	62
ONCE A HOME	63
FLOWERS DON'T FLY	63
HOME IN THE DEEP	63
LEAVING' LOVE BEHIND	63
ONE PERFECT ROSE...	64
ALL THAT MATTERS	65
EVERY MORNING...	66
EXITS	67
STILL	68
PINHOLES IN FABRIC	69
THERE WERE BLACK COWBOYS...?	71
THIS SHOULD HAVE BEEN PAGE 1...	72
THE LAST PAGE	72
A WHISTLE-STOP	73
EROS AGAPE LOVE – SEASON 4	74

LESSON 8 – OPENING MY DOOR	76
MEMORIES OF THE GARDEN	76
JUST BREATHE…	77
… A MESSAGE	77
TREE FEATHERS IN OUR FOREST BED	78
REALLY	78
SWEET CHOCOLATE	79
WARM WEATHER REPORT…CLICK CLICK	80
FULL…	81
LOVE WINS…	82
SISTERS…	83
HEROES GOT NO GUARANTEE OF TOMORROW	85
NO SIMPLE PROMISE	86
UNSPOKEN…	87
STORIES FOR HOT SUMMER NIGHTS…	88
WE SING THE "SONG OF THE VILLAGE"	89
DECLARATION OF INDEPENDENCE…	91
TOMORROW…	92
SEE ME…!	93
REFLECTION ON "SEE ME…!"	94
AMEN!?"	95
WOMAN'S LIB	96
ESCAPE FROM CAPE COAST CASTLE…	98
BIRTHRIGHTS… MY REFLECTION IS MY HISTORY	99
REFLECTION ON "BIRTHRIGHTS…"	101
DARK ADDICTION	102
STILL SMOKING	102
"WILD BUTTERFLIES"	103
COCO'S KINGDOM	104
CHEERLEADERS IN APRONS	104
HOME AGAIN	107
PSALM OF THE HEART-FORTRESS…	108

ONLY FROM HERE…	110
REPRISE	112
CHAPTER 2	113
NUN'S PRAYER (LOVE LOST)	114
JUNKMAN	115
"A LETTER TO GOD"	116
THE WORD	118
FORGIVENESS	119
ONE PERFECT DAY – SEASON 5	120
SHAKESPEARE	122
DIAMOND STUDS…	123
UNDER CONSTRUCTION	123
REFLECTION ON "UNDER CONSTRUCTION"	124
BICENTENNIAL STUDENT REBELLION	125
REFLECTION ON "BICENTENNIAL STUDENT REBELLION"	126
LESSON FOUR	127
WHEN…?	128
LESSON TWO	128
A PASSION FOR LIVING	129
BURNING EMBERS…	129
ALONE	130
INSPIRATION	130
CHULA… (PRETTY BABY)	131
REFLECTION ON "PRETTY BABY"	132
"PARADISE LOST…".	133
AN XX AUTOBIOGRAPHY	134
SIMPLE PLEASURES	134
STORY OF A FREE BEAR	135
CRISTO REDENTOR…	137
MY "NOT SO ACCIDENTAL BLESSING"	138
ONE GRAIN OF SAND…	140
HEART'S WORK…	141

WHEN THE WELL RUNS DRY…	143
FALLEN PETALS…	144
SUICIDE…	145
LESSON FIVE	146
SANGUINE REMINDERS	147
REFLECTION ON "SANGUINE REMINDERS"	148
ONLY UNIQUE	149
LESSON SIX -> NOT WORKING…	150
MY DREAM HAS A NAME	151
LOST AND FOUND…	152
THE KISS	153
COUNTRY GIRL	154
PRECAUTIONARY MEASURES…	155
IN MY SKIN…	156
WHAT MAKES YOU THINK…	157
"PLANTING ORCHARDS"	158
FOOLISHNESS	158
HONEY…	159
WHEN DREAMS MAY END…	159
WON SENTENCE E-MAIL	160
PREAMBLE TO LIFE	160
FAN MALE…	160
FAMILIAR…	161
NO SCULPTING LOVE…	161
PARADISE AWAITING	161
ALMOST MISTAKEN IDENTITY…	162
"I AM" TO A WOODLAND QUEEN	162
COLOR PALETTES ON THE HILLSIDE	163
DAYDREAMER	163
HEART'S LOST AND FOUND	164
SHARING YOUR LIFE…	164
ON-TIME ARRIVAL…	165

CONSPIRACY NOT TO LOVE...	166
PARK DANCING...	167
ANGELS I MUST HAVE SEEN...	168
REFLECTION ON "ANGELS I MUST HAVE SEEN..."	169
IT WAS NEVER LOVE...	170
WHO WAS SHE?	171
ALMOST PARADISE... (DEMENTIA)	172
PERFECT VISION AFTER 50 YEARS...	173
LIES	174
TRUTH	174
WEDDING DANCE...	174
FATUOUS	175
YESTERDAY'S FEAST...	176
SMILES REPRISE	176
"NOT UNIQUELY YOURS..."	177
"A MOIST INKY REPLY..."	178
BE NOT DISMAYED...	179
"HALLMARK LOVER"	180
LINT	180
TICKS IN YOUR KNICKERS...	181
"IF THIS IS NOW... NOW WHAT?"	182
SINGING ~~THE BLUES~~ COUNTRY WESTERN	183
MESSENGER	183
DÉJÀ ~~VU~~ EAR	183
BACK TO THE BEGINNING...	183
25 YEAR STALEMATE...	184
THE WINK	184
ANASTOMOSIS ERSATZ	184
LOST STOCKINGS	185
AAAHHHH...!	185
I DARED TO TELL YOU...	185
SURVIVOR... NOT YET COMPLETE...A REFLECTION	186

FROM THE OUTSIDE IN	187
A SIMPLE "XOXO" PRAYER	187
REJOICE	188
MY TIME HAS COME...	189
NEW FRUIT IN THE GARDEN	190
THE SCENT OF YOU...	191
NOTES TO MY READERS...	192
INNER CIRCLE – SEASON 6	192
MUSE	194
SKINNY DIPPING IN THE MOONLIGHT	194
EN PLEIN AIR	195
THE FIRST SEASONS... MY EARLY YEARS	196
HISTORY FOR MY UNDOING	197
AND SO NOW I WRITE	199
IT'S JUST A D__K THANG...	200
POET'S DEMENTIA	201
I'D SING YOU A SONG...	202
BUCKET LIST...	203
LIFE'S PUZZLE...	204
RUNNING TOO SLOW	205
ON ROCKS BELOW	205
APOLOGIES...	206
PHOTOS IN A SHOE BOX	206
INDELIBLE...	207
NO LONGER A DREAM DEFERRED...DARE!	209
FIRST SEASONS – LIFE'S IMPROVISATIONS	211
CAT'S PAWS	213
ALL THAT MATTERS	214
DIAMOND STUDS...	214
IF I AM YOUR SEA...	215
JUST BREATHE...	215
MESMERIZED	216

A MUSICAL LABYRINTH…	217
FALL REPOSE…	217
LIFE A REPRISE – JUST TO BE LOVED!	218
YESTER-MOMENTS NOW REVISITED…	219
SHOUT	220
WAITING ON YOU REPRISE	222
FALL REPOSE REPRISE OF TREE FEATHERS	223
AND NOW I SLEEP	223
ALZHEIMER	224
FALLEN ANGEL	224
SALVATION FOR THE NEXT GENERATION	225
1600 PENN 2016	226
AND THEN I SMILED…	226
INTENTIONAL LIVING	227
THE NEXT SEASONS – LOOKING AHEAD	229
A GIFT	229
THE JOURNEY IS NOT OVER	230
LETTING GO	231
SALTY TEARS	232
QUESTIONS FROM MY READERS…	233
ANSWERS TO YOUR QUESTIONS - INTRODUCTION	234
WHEN HEART'S SURRENDER	249
SO, WHAT DID I LEARN…?	250
POSTSCRIPT	251

The weaving of silk tapestries – as
if by clever timeless artisans..., woven
nightly for sunrise completion, to be
covered in dew for fresh eyes to discover
in surprise...
Be in awe.

Sunday Morning Worship

Looking upon endless and inspiring, I set out to be in
fearful awe of spirit-filled wonders birthed for faithful
adventurous souls at a daybreak worship

The walk is swift to explore at lowest tides an unseen
terrain far from shore and never to be repeated –
replete with sand-dollars in the arms of kelp
outstretched to capture a fallen treasure

In adoration of other worldly beauty – a promised
paradise awaiting, but out of view, the first steps to
wisdom fearfully carry celebrants outward and back to
solid foundations of stone

There will be no outrunning "living water" purposefully
wetting dry sand beyond the place I stand
with a promise to cover all in need, I too retreat
mesmerized and entranced by fearsome power and I
am silenced to observe the work of an Invisible Hand…

Unrelenting of a promise, a slate is erased and wiped
smooth and clean – now invisible, the steps across this
perfection, as if forgiving me for an intrusion with
immersive ablutions

With rumbling restraint awaiting my wary retreat, the
table on which I have given adoration in sacrifice is
reclaimed for the next daybreak morning worship

I now go with grace and peace received

Reflection on Sunday Morning...

The Sand Dollar Legend is an Easter and Christmas favorite which tells a story that includes the five slits representing the wounds of Christ when on the cross. The Easter lily with a star in the middle represents the star of Bethlehem and on the back is the outline of a Poinsettia, the Christmas flower.

Tears of a rose...

Today as I walked in the rain, I saw a rose moving to and fro with the impact of drops upon its petals.

As I stared at this beauty, I knew it would soon be severed from its stem to grace the whim of some fickle beauty, or to dot an eye – a boutonnière for some princely charmer.

Or, perhaps, it would be celebrated as a centerpiece on some table to witness a hearty meal.

But, for now, raindrops ran between the petals like rivers, and fell to the ground.

I fancied them tears.

First Lines... in the diary of "A rainy day sister..."

– Page 1

Today, I caught a drop of rain on my face and seasoned it with a salty tear.

I colored it with dark background and gave it a home on my cheek, where it called to a friend whom I welcomed in kind.

Sunlight Prisms

>Today, raindrops are prisms for sunshine
>Each affirming the physics of "joy colors"
>Yellow, Red, and Blue on the boudoir walls
>And seemingly, also Pinks that color your cheeks
>That now remember the recent night in day's light

Awesome - A Celestial Sigh...

>Light years behind and still millennia ahead traveling
>>on waves through a universe curving past near
>>missed planets, and celestial rocks to arrive
>>amid streams of yellow, red and blue fellow-
>>beams all in search of an audience.
>
>Today's quietly waiting worshipers whispering and gasping
>>at a temporal and fancied perpetual gift of inspired
>>sunsets changing to darkness, with strumming, and
>>celebrating beneath cloudless skies – beside
>>competing lighted piles of beach wood.
>
>While friends and lovers in repose gaze above.
>And others, reckon the plot of a show ten million years
>>in the making as a celestial lightshow before black
>>curtains – to be admired behind lenses and savored
>>and saved – just this instance – as each star
>>surrenders its memory to words pregnant with
>>meaning – beautiful, "amazing" and other single
>>exclamations of "Awesome!
>
>All without concern that this wonderous engagement is
>>NOW and Now NEVERMORE.

Finding Faith

I have taken baby steps, sometimes falling on my face.
With pride, I hasten to call it challenging and the thrill of exploring.
SHe turns the earth, calling it a day and expands the universe beyond knowing.

I think my thoughts profound and label them BRILLIANCE.
So, with "great" intellect, I launch mighty ships, call the world flat and write the anthems of nations.
SHe speaks a single word and calls into being black holes beyond the edge of Hubble's view.

I erect buildings surpassing small mountains and look from my penthouse at passing clouds.
With chest expanded and my head elevated, I proclaim myself mighty.
SHe smiles at me with love and hangs more stars in the skies.

I think myself unique among the millions and most worthy of praise.
With hammer and chisel, I inscribe my own name in stone above doorways and on cornerstones, to be remembered forever.
SHe knows the hairs of my head, calls me "Son" and promises to forget me never.

And now that my creations crumble, and wind and water erase my name,
I have removed me from the equation, finally knowing immutable truth of laws even here.
SHe offers mustard seed faith accompanied by mercy and unending love to conquer fear.

No longer relying on "just me" to control my life, I understand that what matters most – was given freely to dry tears from worldly eyes.
All because SHe nailed my pain to a cross with promises to forgive even the greatest deceits and lies.

I have taken baby steps, sometimes falling on my face.
So, now mustard greens are grown for the sake of seeds, as a small reminder of my gifts in grace.

In Awe

Awake to endless and eternal and be in awe
Of wonders the universe births for creative beings

Laborers working feverishly in moonlight without knowing the sunrise outcomes… All orchestrated by flowing energetic streams into present times…, maybe by fate.
Be in awe.

Toiling to create art arriving from an "endless SOURCE", with only a universe's purpose to guide diligent instincts and deft members…
Be in awe.

The weaving of silk tapestries – as if by clever timeless artisans…, woven nightly for sunrise completion, to be covered in dew for fresh eyes to discover in surprise…
Be in awe.

Contemplate at the base of a tree – clover leaves counting three in hopes of being four, or even five. Vines and moss hanging from branches to tethered leaves, of sticky silk to capture – each a unique design – framed in perfect view…
Be in awe.

Walk in beds of flowers, between giant ferns and up-ended logs of magical woods…, into a gallery beyond mankind's design and art. For discovery – a creation and revelation perfectly timed for Elves and Fairies to rediscover at mornings' light. Join in gladness, with a joy-enabled heart…
Be in awe.

Awake…, to a new Morning's Glory and rejoice!

Crystal Kisses…

Though you reside in a place distant – now too far to abide my kisses

My table still boasts memories of your warmth and recent presence in near view

On foreign crystal, ruby lips are clearly outlined atop an adoring rim

Where no ordinary goblet was worthy – your nobility, and beauty required much more

To receive softest caresses, on best offerings – your touch, too sublime, and nothing less

I now contemplate the discernable peaks and valleys left as memories

Holding a fragile stem and nearing a lingering fragrance, I drain the last drops of wine

Nectar anxious for your return – an inferior surrogate for what you bring and leave behind, brings joy to

Lips that happily adore and are satisfied for this single moment in time

A Perfect Pair

At morning's light, I awake to pillows covered in silk,
    announcing your workday departure from
Crumpled sheets, and an accidental treasure left behind
    reminds me of wonders
At rest, beneath down in morning's light, with no kinship to
    any pea or mattress fable
A silver post, garnets, a lone diamond, to remind me of lovely
    ears
That tickled when I blew into them softly – squirming with
    giggles as if escape was possible, but NOT – sweet ears
Warmed when I whispered love poems and sonnets to them –
    pushing against a heart's haven
Acutely listening and pressed to soft hairs, hearing "heart-
    speak" of love, and
Energies connected to this twin gone missing, for the day trip in
    your purse
Hoping for your return to search for a missing treasure, tucked
    safely in my pocket
And now on this eve, we wait ready by the door, to reunite a
    perfect pair
One, come lately to hear and another to partake of love

Dogma

Doctrines and Rules are the
fences and walls to protect
"insecure and not sure"
How IS your mind today?
Practicing high-jumps?

Lighting Fire to Ready Tinder

You never meant to change a mind or life with what
 seemed inconsequential conversation
About lines, art, and perception of things, paint, and
 fabric clinging to a backdrop
Being explained to some upturned and eager face –
 black velvet skin and brooding eyes
Then voilà! Something new was born in an eager
 mind and a hungry spirit
You never meant to change a path by explaining how
 some canvas calling itself creative
Would cover some wall in a place never
 remembered by an inattentive passersby
Or that it would imagine some beauty in oil to
 demand a high price for its capture
Then voilà! Something beautiful was created – an
 eager mind and a discerning eye
You never meant to change the world by changing a
 direction - almost imperceptible
With your smile authentic and gleeful, telling of
 history, nuance and connecting to this day's
 reality
Or real meaning beyond the aesthetic, to open
 worlds of creation and new vision for what
 could be
Then voilà! Something exciting happened – a union
 from layered brushstrokes to birth new life
You never meant to change a direction, or be a guide
 to new stars well past the known universe
Or create a new place past the unimaginable, to
 arrive at new understanding near inspirational
When you explained to a young and ready mind that
 now remembers the hour as if today
Then voilà! The story that you never meant to write,
 or to repeat was born and still lives in me
You never meant to be remembered for an
 unplanned instant that changed a life
Although you never meant to be a treasured
 memory that changed perceptions and views
Nor meant to change me, never knowing what I
 could achieve or where I have been because of
 you

Continued...

Then voilà! A new creature evolved, and now, I
    thank you for what I have become
You never meant to be remembered, or to change
    my world, but I vow never to forget you
Now, you are my legend - giving first life to brushes
    and acrylics for my own creations
Though you may never know, I follow your example
    of bringing smoldering tender to life
When voilà! Your greatest gift now mine, is shared -
    bringing heat to an eager mind. Fire!

Reflection on "Light Fire to Ready Tender"

A good friend of mine shared the story of what I believe to be a very special event.

During the course of redecorating a home, she had what she considered to be a casual but fun conversation with a young man about a painting – a very large abstract that was being hung.

After being delivered, the painting was leaning against the wall that would become its' final home. She stood back admiring it and saying how "cool" she thought it was. One of the young movers, came to stand beside her and quietly said, "I don't understand art. I don't get it. What is it supposed to be? "

Her response was, "The beauty of art is that it means different things to different people. You will see something that I may not. What do you see?"

He paused briefly and then walked over to the painting for a closer inspection. After a moment he began a critique of the work. She immediately noticed a shift in his demeanor.

With hand gestures and facial expressions, he launched into a dialog with her. But almost as if musing to himself, he explained, "I see a woman giving birth to her child! "

She was impressed, amazed and frankly stunned at the insight of this quiet, seemingly shy young man. In the space of a few moments he delivered a critique with aplomb and sureness.

Continued...

Pleased with himself, he also decided that not everyone would be able to see what he so keenly observed. His eyes now had a certain new life within, accompanied by a confident smile.

Her comment to me was that as she walked away, she was thinking "What just happened?"

What she believed with some delight, was a casual encounter, I believed was a life-altering event for both of them. In my opinion, she had just helped him to write an unforeseen chapter into his new autobiography.

I never really know who is watching or listening when I do or say something. We are unaware, more often than not, of the impact we have on some unknown observer – the woman at the desk; the man driving the bus; the children playing in the street.

With that knowledge, I consider and take responsibility for my actions and the words I speak. I hope that I am making a difference when I am authentic, kind and loving.

A Perfect Petal...

>Gathered petals – yellow, pink and red
>From a thousand rose blossoms
>Placed on a come-hither bed
>Creating a potpourri of smells
>Remembrances of intimacies
>Wait for rediscovery
>Knowing that the most beautiful petal
>Is not to be defrocked but adored
>When you lay beside me in blissful repose
>In the bed I have picked for you

Hope's Arrival...

At days-end, furtive glances into empty mailboxes with
    the expectancy of word gifts weigh on my heart.
In down-time hours of "not the one" overcasts eyes and
    encourages endless refresh of everything but
    hope.
And now, at last stealthy scripts appear, posing as dots
    and haiku, and casual ramblings where I search for
    single words to elicit sighs and happy release.
That one line among a queued list should summon
    to a face, a light-year star, gives new meaning
    to extraordinary!!!
So much so, that doors ajar, leak brightness into
    nighttime, waking flowers to bloom, thinking
    spring and days arrival eminent...
Erasing shadows and gloom fueled by simple letters on a
    screen to wake my slumbered fearful heart.
Brings renewal to lines of poetry with thoughts of you.
I wait now at the desktop hoping for another small
    gift to brighten the encroaching despair, of
    another 14-hour day in battle-dress, 7,000
    miles away.
Let there be a word or two you might have forgotten
    to add... Another "I love you..."
So now I wait with hope.

Holidays...

Holidays are reasons for celebration.
Your smiles are my holidays and I celebrate your kisses,
every day.

The Path to Prayer

Falling from heights to my knees, I am prone for tearful pleading.
Laying in submission and total surrender to a loving force, whose energy is not my own, and of which I have little understanding,
save that my groans and words are received, and deliver meaningful outcomes filled with unmerited goodness - grace
and mercy, for which I respond with joy and gratitude.
In the hands of the "Potter", when shards become vessels of changed wine from water-for-life gifts, because
my pleas are heard with love. Then in joyous relief I shout, "AMEN!"

I am transformed.

Wisdom

I recognized stupid,
when wisdom arrived
It was my new normal
But it was your everyday
Thanks for stopping by…

Fear Reframed

Now tightness in my chest and a nighttime chill attend perspiration on my skin.
What was I thinking when my words claimed brute courage and strength, speaking my truth?

Now a heartbeat in my ears rivals the club's bass speakers, only amplified.
What was I thinking when anger of the moment and pride inspired me? Now the hand clenched to a fist clings desperately to a lifeline from EMT. What was I thinking when thoughts of anger justified plans to still truth and steal love from the birth of something beautiful together for the sake of being right – in the moment?

Now, if only my heart I could slow and quiet so no one would know of my reproach.
What was I thinking when I left home, imagining that today was just another day?

Like no other I have known, I would give my all for just one more day that may never come.
What was I thinking when I heated words to fill the room – a vacuum for forgiveness? My fear and prayer for "just a bad dream" that could end when I shut my eyes. What was I thinking when life was about me, without consequence, or compromise?

Hear a heart's cry of "forgiveness...?" Now I am praying that coming-home-grace and mercy are in ample supply today.

In Need of New Beginnings

    Me

    War

    Rage

    Rancor

    Suspicion

    Burning Buildings

    Weapons for Killing

    Stop NOW to reframe the thinking

    NOW a Time for Healing

    Hearts for Filling

    No Searing Flames

    No Hatred

    No Anger

    No War

    Justice

    Peace

    Us

Love's Re-TREAT

Warm!
Sweet and
Sticky

Honey for licking
Fleeting Moments
On a clock ticking
Blinks in eternity

A memory valued
More than retweeting
Eager for repeating
No More re-treating

More sticky honey
Warm and
Sweet

Another week

No Longer a Secret Garden…

Laying in innocence in crumpled silk beneath my gaze, you know
That inviting me to follow your curves will lead me invariably and
    maybe not so innocently to your smile
Whose arrival will raise the temperature at my core
By measures of exploding stars being sucked into places where light
    does not escape, just as you will not
From an embrace that pulls our energies to spaces moist, warm, and
    ready for new seasons of growth
Springing to life in heart-spaces and places that we will call our "new
    arboretum for loving…"
While you lay in soft meadows of your kingdom I will stand eager to
    hear your bidding…
"Come!" you will say, and I will hasten to you side.
In joy and love, I will obey

Continuing Diary... of "A rainy day sister..."

Entry Jan 21 1968 – Page 2

Today the sun came out and the heat from its rays seem to pierce deep within my soul to warm cool recesses and to light the walls that will radiate heat in later hours.

I smiled broadly throughout the morning and looked at midday to the mirror, to compose myself for an excursion into town.

The tears of darker times were gone, but salty trails remain.

Perhaps they are reminders of times that could return. Or, maybe they are personal road signs back to bad times. But this is not a path I choose today, and I wipe away the markers.

My sadness is a recent memory, but Joy will be my constant companion today.

Water Lilies or Love NOTES

Water lilies on a pond
very much resemble at dawn
unexpected love notes
left in all the right places
by some silent hand.
And I only hope that tomorrow
there will be more lilies
and less spaces.

No Edits on Yesterday

There's no repeat…no repeal…no replay.
We've talked about the things we would redo in youth vs what age would have us undo…if we could. Having written, the cursor moves on…and no amount of backspacing will undo the words I've written, or the poems I've committed to memory, and etched with my life, or shared with **YOU** who came "**BY INVITATION ONLY**" – to be part of my saga, drama, or comedy.

And even though, I "could'a, would'a, should'a", I wouldn't change a thing TODAY.
There's no repeat…no repeal…no replay.

All my past decisions are permanent and will not be removed by repeated washings or attempts to remove… If your participation is something you'd like to deny…, I apologize for having lured you to my stage, venue or neighborhood for a moment of regret or joy.

If I was invited to be part of **YOUR** poetry, I hope I've made the cut and remain a stanza, a line or even a word in **YOUR** book that made a difference or created some poignant memory that justifies this poem.

And even though, I "could'a, would'a, should'a", I wouldn't change a thing TODAY.
There's no repeat…no repeal…no replay.
If you've asked **ME** to remove **YOU** from

my memories. The answer is short and sweet…,
"**NO**" says it all. It's not my call, and just barely my words. Your appointment to help write this story was scheduled long ago, so you couldn't have been late if you tried…

And even if I could, erasing you would surely tear the fabric and leave a gaping hole that no new word, phrase or stanza would fill. You see, you've made a difference to me. So, I won't be using Magic Rub to **PRETEND** that "**IT**" never happened, or "**YOU**" never mattered.

It **IS** because of what **WAS**, and my life could only have been different if I was a different **ME** and you a different **YOU**. But we're not, so "**HERE I AM**," "**THERE YOU ARE**," and in **HIS** perfect timing we meant something to each other **THEN**. And, my **NOW** will always hold your memory.

Continued…

And even though, I "could'a, would'a, should'a", I wouldn't change a thing TODAY. There's no repeat…no repeal…no replay.

The wisdom of ages now tells me that when I was young, had I been given the chance of rewriting my short past, I would surely have rushed to **EDIT**, and the regretful events would lie scattered as discard on cutting room floors.

But now, with so much behind – a winding path stretching to the ***hindsight horizon***, how could I change a single thing knowing that with some miniscule **REDO** or **REVIEW** I might not pass this way again. You surely could have been on another road - a memory that never was, or I a **CHOICE** you could have decided not to make. I would miss you. With such a costly option, I could never change a thing. *What would the play be without Othello…Ophelia?*

And even 'though, I "could'a, would'a, should'a", I wouldn't change a thing TODAY. There's no repeat…no repeal…no replay.

So, there can be no rewrites or going home on roads already traveled. But I have memories of what was for a moment a "**HERE AND NOW** of **GREAT IMPORTANCE**" and filled with **REAL FEELINGS** for a season that words were good enough to capture. Now **MY SEASONS** have passed and are indelibly written in these pages for my children to read.

My message and conviction is "Make the choice not to change a thing until you know the consequences of **NOW** and **THEN** (a now, way back when…)
If you doubt what I am saying, rip out this page and try to forget that you ever read it.

So, even though, I "could'a, would'a, should'a" written something else, been something more, or

somehow loved differently, I wouldn't change a thing…. **NOW that I know about consequences!**

There's no repeat…no repeal…no replay…
I wouldn't change a thing **TODAY**.
There'll be no repeat…no repeal…no replay.

Now and Then...

Smiles are like jewels and a simple response now, on beautiful days at Normandy Beach
Where warriors traversed an ocean in service to freedom - there to die in stained sand
Now, but never forgetting the fallen lifeblood, peace is a jewel no longer lying in wait but an homage to faith
Now discovered by lovers of internal sunshine looking for parted clouds for an explosion of rays
Now blessed with grace and finding it, an inheritance is discovering unexpected revelations, as searches
for historical truth reveal treasures abiding in plain sight – that grand-Père was here
Now ideals proclaim the "Good News" that need not be completely understood
That just a mustard seed concept, where so many have died to give life is where freedom now reigns
Now is an expanding understanding and appreciation that the greatest treasure and surprises are LIFE informing,
LIFE affirming, about existing and becoming – erupting through parted lips of passersby
Now some looking feverishly for revelation will find others, also searching and finding ultimate love wrapped
in a smile, an unearned gift of grace in reflection to one another and grown from the inside out
telling of "no greater love"
Now they are jewels in simple response on grateful days at Normandy Beach
A simple smile for what has gone before as the ultimate gift to one another

Merci

Incurable...

I have figured it out – infected with your love and in
    need of no cure.

Blades of grass are now greener, skies bluer and
    stars shine brighter.

I float into the air, unable to keep my feet on the
    ground.

Candles burn hotter leaving wax puddles on counters, like
    breadcrumbs, after nightly romance and moonlight
    skinny dripping on private beaches.

Spreading quickly through my being, I smile frequently and
    for no apparent reason at friends, strangers, and past
    enemies now bosom friends.

No longer in denial, my diagnosis is "smitten" with a
    virus of our making.

I am giving it back to you, to share with me as a
    chronic condition.

For this, I offer a loving heart in need of no cure.

Friends

Before...
I always worried that Life would be too much to handle, but now that my life is filled with helpers – my friends, there is no doubt that I'll be able to scale the Rockies – and bridge canyons like skipping across sidewalk cracks.

I can conquer all of life's challenges.
...Now that we are together as one – a family loyal to my endeavors, a cheering section to my successes – lovers of the real ME...

A positive reality is now on my side and I know the person in the mirror – a friend who smiles back at me with pride – a reflection on my side, eternally.

My friends are the lovers of who I am and what I will someday BE

Before we walked on the beaches holding hands – a strange duo, trio and quartet – all singing, dancing, laughing and crying together, I never knew about emotional truth and not denying nor fearing what hid within.

Now, with special ones in my world, I recognize the strength in the reflection – the REAL ME.

Reflection on Friends

My first primer on friendship came from my daughter. I watched how she bonded to her mom and to the girls she adopted as sisters through her school years. The word I use to describe the relationships she developed is "faithful."

Through the years, I have seen her bonds with sisters deepen and grow. I have observed the same types of relationships with my sisters and women who have touched my life as they fostered a network of authentic supporters.

I am convinced at this point that women are far more blessed than men with the ability to build friendships and to maintain them for a lifetime.

In my life, I have had only two men for whom I felt this connection. It is a blessing that I would multiply a hundredfold if I knew how to recreate the fate that brought us together.

You Shine...

Flowers and I stand ready, outside your door.

With your appearance, we will raise our faces
To smile at you...

When you depart, we will turn back to the sun
To await your return...

Anthem

A personal anthem "for the end"

I sang a song beneath your window
But your light went out,
and my voice fell silent.
Your light glowed no longer...
No more do I sing...

Oh say, can you see...?

To NIKKI

I came to hear you sing my praises -
You punctured my bubble.

I came to hear you speak of me -
You plugged my ears.

I came to bask in the reflection of me in your eyes -
You turned out the lights.

I came to pick your brain -
You stilled my lips.

I came to learn from you -
You handed me a mirror and said, "Lesson One."

Reflection on "To Nikki"

In the 70's, Nikki Giovanni was just Nikki to me. I played her record "Like a Ripple on a Pond" until I wore away the grooves. When I couldn't afford a new needle, I lightened the weight, and played the cuts again and again. Eventually, the albums died and were reborn many times on new vinyl.

I continued buying albums until 20th century science freed me with the invention of binary digits on Compact Discs.

Through the years, as I learned some of the harder lessons she taught, I came to the realization that Nikki was more than a poet. In and out of the classroom, she was a counselor, a friend, a lover of humanity, a social anthropologist, a historian and a keen observer of life's joy and anguish.

She, Maya and Langston have re-defined the word poet for me to be more than architects to rhyming words. We are painters of insights through rippled-glass and mirrors with a universe in view for all with eyes to see.

For all you have done, to inspire me and others who follow in your footsteps, I say thank you.

Casting Seeds to the Aire…

I looked among the flowers in the garden for a radiant blossom
To my delight, the search was short, for I found you sitting
There at our tree beneath the scrawled 1-4-3, you turned your face
An upward glance, like a flower seeking the sun, and smiled brightly in my
    direction
Immediately, I knew that you were about your meditation of pushing seeds
    of love Into the air that surrounded you - drifting off on whiffs of lilac
    and roses, to lead others to gardens of their choosing, to find their
    lovers awaiting beneath "I-LOVE-YOU (1-4-3)".
There, to behold and be held in joy, in the act of meditating and creating
    seeds of their own…

A New Day Dawning...

Sunlight pushing away darkness
Parting lids with clouds receding
Cleansing tear ducts that wash away fear and regret
Opening a heart for loving and giving
Accepting goodness in place of hate
Breathing in peace to force out the anger
Building up what others have torn down
Reaching out to lead the way
Arms spread wide for embracing
Dropping Pride by the way…, a side that has no place
Letting go of control in preparation for spiritual guidance
A new day dawning is filled with hope

Who was she?

She was a flower in the desert – a cactus flower
surrounded by barren hills, dust and heat…,
She bloomed and blossomed and brought joy into
my life.

She stood straight and proud in a land of multicolored
dullness and dwarfed the Eiffel Tower.
In repose, she shamed the Louvre with her artfully wrought
ebony features.

She created masterfully correct concepts and was more
insightful than the great philosophers.
Plato and Aristotle would do well to compare her naps to
Buddha.

She was the definition and true meaning of beauty.
She was the mold of greatness, the cast of proper,
the graduate of smart and right, and she taught me love.

Who was she?
My Love…, it was you.

"Evasive..."

You ask, "Why friendship...?"
And I answer in poems that tell, of loneliness you've filled...
Like a blade of grass pushing aside leaves to expose its newness.
Alone it is unseen from high mountains until one friend, and still
another adds color to a blanket of green. And flowers of varied hues
and colors spread a patchwork quilt between the horizon's edges.
It is a colorful bed that gives me pillows for repose, and a soft resting
place that forgives my curves and lack of constancy.

You ask, "Why loving...?"
I respond with allegories and metaphors that speak of 'oneness'...
And I say, loving with you reminds me greatly of spring's feverish
eruption of new life and smelling lilacs on a summer's breeze.
I whisper that our feelings are like cool spring water parading in
droplets and swells across parched lips. Then, I tell you that your
voice is like the harmony of birds signaling a prelude to rebirth after
the snows are gone. Our feelings are night creatures serenading the
stars on summer nights.

Finally, you ask, "Why me...?"
Your eyes must surely have read the answers in my face...
Because I and you are reflections of our best parts.
Because we were meant to be, like an oyster and pearl.
Because now after 53 years, when I sit on the beach remembering us
and thinking of you, my heart still smiles.
And I know you feel it too.
You are "the One."

RUBY

You gave feeling and color to words I remember clearly, even though now you're gone
Without you, they were only mechanisms of "talk" and "write," but sitting at your side listening to family stories, they were history lessons
Not just fables where you were the main character, the main observer, or just the main perpetrator of stories retold on occasions to transform the nights, and to unlock my mind to "creative" — giving me hope for my tomorrows
"Once upon a time" is now a short preamble describing your lively times to my children
When your youthful moment was a dance on Chestnut, or a party in Gaslight Square
They were a series of moments in time — followed by another and yet another story
All connected in some way," It seems like just yesterday, when"
You were the main character, the main observer, or just the main perpetrator
In stories retold on so many occasions to mesmerize me beneath streetlights at night, and to unlock my soul to "vivid mindscapes" – giving me visions for my tomorrows
I use your words now, to spice languid evenings with your life's seasoned appreciation, to be handed down by your children
To recount, to your grandchildren – my children, family stories, and even
What seemed like fables where you were the main character, the main observer or just the main perpetrator of the most unbelievable antics, before raising four children
Alone and unlocking our hearts to the possibilities we each possessed for tomorrows
In vicarious retellings of your visions, histories and "family forests" not family trees
I sit on the porch, on the deck or near the ocean, painting brilliant mindscapes that entertain
On full moonlit nights — I mesmerize my children with the "Grandma Ruby Stories"
That begin with "Once upon a time, when we used to be in Saint Louis, and
It seems like just yesterday," when "Grandma" told this story to me
So I could tell it to you, and you could retell it to your children, knowing that
In her stories, she lives forever, to entrance and unlock the best parts of our hearts and minds

A Finish Line Review

Once upon a time, I stood on my timeline at twenty-five, filled with counterfeit wisdom.

I looked toward the future, stretching beyond the horizon to see eternity as a starlit sky above the trees.

Now, forty years later, a mandated retrospect is a clear view from the front porch, back to a youthful face.

He is looking my way with no recollection of history or wisdom for sharing – just a handsome youth staring at the sky.

I return a smile and look skyward myself, with new revelation that my time here is like a single moonbeam.

I know now, that it is almost time to leave this familiar place to begin a great adventure that I no longer dread.

Looking to the stars now, I have no great wisdom to share but I am open for the spiritual awakening that awaits me.

Wondering what I will be seeing from there to here.
In that future, I will surely look to my past and review my time among worldly souls.

That eulogy will be to the poor vision of youth, but a proclamation of lifelong JOYS!

There will be announcements of a new star –
"Perfected Sight and Pure Delight."

My timeline will be endless, and hopefully my wisdom will become threads of "the fabric" –
for your discovery.

Next Peace

We plan the reality of our days starting quietly on
    the deck, with coffee in hand
The place where the ocean waves break on rocks to
    create a personal rainbow
Watching the new sun usher the stars and moon
    from the sky to darkness in need of pale light
Each is a day in review followed by leisurely
    moments drinking in the sounds of peace
What could be better than this - hearing the waves
    below talking to rocks and a whispered retreat
As the tide rushes in to moisten sandy roots and the
    sun departs for its nightly repose as tiny lights
    appear above
They are stars we know - that see us in the company
    of a candle's glow and think it a gifted fallen star
What comes next is more of the same, followed by
    what comes next in peace

by Ronald Montgomery

The "Freedom Bird" was the flight that took soldiers to a R&R destination, or back to the World at the end of a tour of duty, or earlier if the flight back *home* was an 8-mil body bag.

My Bedside Garden...

Yesterday, a carnation was taken from the garden to grace a bedside table for one perfect day.
This is what it lived for and no day would ever be the same.
Even the best days that followed would be withered imitations of this moment of *first perfection.*

Today in a vase, a rose blushed and its color and fragrance filled the room to bursting and slowly began to dissipate.
What it has not been told, is that the garden anxiously awaits reports of "the smile" so that they will know the impact of this beauty...and the marvel at the look of wonder.
This would be a high standard they might never know if not chosen on just the right day..., and my days are few I know

Tomorrow, a violet, or trumpet lily may provide a perfect message and achieve "the look and smile."
Or, perhaps it will be a tulip, or a dandelion that too, could blossom in its sweetest aroma and fade.
Surely this would be the moment of its greatest admiration, and beauty to see and enjoy.

For Someday, the garden beauties wait to be part of a special moment, or a memory – to be admired on the tabletop garden next to my bed.
And for now, I too wait for a day of perfection when I will be picked from this garden and "the look of the Master" will tell me that today is my best day of all.

A Wake-up...

179 and a wake-up on a short-timers sheet over
Snap-On Tools images laid to the side in a tent city
And dreaming of the last R and R to Bangkok
But waiting for the real thing back in the "world"
And thinking the best part of me would live to see that day
Another day gone and now an endless 24 to go
With "X's"- beneath one another, knowing
One and a wake-up is the ultimate count
Just one more day to the "Freedom Bird"
And never wanting to have the darker view
I see now – inside and catching an
Eight mil bag ride back to the "World"

> A wake-up no more, because I'm already home

Reflection on "Short-Timer"

My first exposure to the "Short-Timer's Calendar" was in the military during the Vietnam conflict. Even today, it continues to be a daily countdown of the time left before a warrior can *rotate back* (go home) to the United States (*the World*), or when ETS (Expiration of Term of Service – a released from active duty) is reached.

The "Snap-Oh Tools Calendar" was frequently the calendar of choice used to count the days. It was well known for the pinup collection of beautiful women adorning each month and was frequently found on the insides of the male soldiers lockers.

R&R (rest and relaxation or rest and recreation) is a trip paid for by the military for soldiers stationed in war zones. During Vietnam for example, it was a single trip during the tour of 12-13 months to places like Bangkok Thailand, Hawaii, or Seoul Korea.

The "Freedom Bird" was the flight that took soldiers to a R&R destination, or back to the *World* at the end of a tour of duty, or earlier if the flight back home was an 8-mil body bag.

I still weep thinking of the thousands of fathers, sons and brother who made such an unjust sacrifice, and returned with no honor in zip locked bags and agent orange.

J' Adore

Moon Over My Amie'

You rise to a status of no other
Higher than friends or wannabe others
Your seat is a quiet place - high above
Constructed not of stone - but clouds
Your Pedestal a naked place
Absent clothes but not of grace
You are valued and worshipped with the stars
For who you are – but not so far...
You are my reachable moon – ma petite Amie
My darling, *You* are kissable Poetry...

IF Poems...Muse-ical

Then...

If poems are flowers, I will write a field of lilies and bouquets of daffodils for you.

If words are notes, then in your name there's a symphony being written with crescendos that climax and codas that return you to me.

If letters are grains of sand, then you shall have a sandy beach to sift between your toes.

If poems are puffs of air, then thoughts of you will billow the sails of valiant men and move great ships to foreign shores.

If poems are pages to a book, then I will fill your ears with a whispered trilogy as you lie sleeping on my chest – where your sighs end chapters and your arms hold me in the plot of your love...

Simple Understanding

The distance between your heart and my head
Isn't timed in moving e(emoji) motions from me to you
Across ether-REAL wisps and bits via Smartphone

Or measured on 3-inch stilettos - sexy in salsa
while I speak feverishly of rising body temperatures
And you expound on kisses, speeding cardio

And it doesn't equate to some mean understanding
When your emotions speak of butterflies and
My mind sees migrating monarchs and explains gastrointestinal flutters

It just points to a different sort of love language
That only you can teach to a willing student
I'm so glad that it's me.

Sunset Celebration

Waves move mountains – as miniscule memories of ocean ranges – now to carpet a path hiding scurrying creatures escaping eager beaks
The work of millennia surrendering to tiny fingers and toes, before smoothing the way to momentary castle creations, to waves or
Catalog crab passages across a moist brow, invisible to crowds contemplating a shared repose on a just visible horizon
They wait for a single moment when you will wrest all from view – waving to adorers a thunderous adieu – through translucent clouds and sometimes sans
Throngs united in awe, surrender you to starry and moonlit space – some in salutatory, but all bidding a fond farewell in awe
An en masse lemming retreat, till your promise of a next evening's embrace draws them here once more

Heart capes

Peaks and gorges mimic distance to head from "heart-speak"

of you to me between walled-off "feeling-enclosures" – to
soft and too sensitive, for "manly", and openness

such difficult dialog for honesty, expedited by "Yes", "No" and
"maybe commitments" to eternal love when peaks and
valleys separate hearts

and fealty seeping between lips longing more for simplicities
of unbridled passions is not embraced but feared

as we lay side by side – a river shared, nourishes and eases
our connections for now – while grass and dandelions grow
on spaces we will call "us"

we now in glowing peace, like spoons and forks in a kitchen
drawer, awaiting the next meal to come – a love feast

in silence contemplate alone still wondering if being
connected at the heart will create a meadow from a valley
and peak

Almost a Woman…

This morning on the anniversary of my birth
I became a woman, all of eighteen
I've determined there'll be no hidden feelings
No holding back, no fears
No evasion of reality
No fakery, no conditional loving or living.
There'll be no giving up
I'll offer honesty from an unconditional me
And be all I was born to be
This is the year and it's going to be different
And it is only just beginning

I look back through the eyes of youth
Coloring the skies bluer, with lenses
That matched my moods
I viewed the world with my rules of
Limitless incomes, infinite outputs and
All the valued things that life offered
That I would never do without

This morning on the anniversary of my birth
I've become a woman, all of forty-eight
Love is never in short supply and waits on me to beckon
I never miss unconditional support for my uniqueness
I am secure knowing that my family and friends have my back.
And that's in the past and in the "Now"
And even in the tomorrows of which I will have many
Some things would never change. I will always be me
This year, it's all gonna be different
And it's just beginning

Since time is passing and feelings are in the open but shielded
Fears are in control and reality is put into perspective
Honesty, unconditional loving and living are my mottoes, and
Giving up holds no attraction and a
unique me is as happy as can be

Continued…

This morning on the anniversary of my birth
My wings are spread to embrace all the years to eighty-eight
Today, remembering the excitement of the first kiss
The joys of friendship and connections – lovers, family and friends
All just the prelude to a symphony still being written and played
Amid fireworks and pyrotechnics, I remember a night
As "Homecoming Queen" I was all the envy
Brash sureness and high spirits lifted me to mountain tops
All these things I'll be remembering as I move to the next stage
And this year in all its glory as I remember the times behind
I am looking forward to all that will be – I can only be me
This year, it's going to be different
And it's only just beginning

Rough Spots

Sometimes getting over the rough spots is like stepping over the cracks in a sidewalk.

At other times it feels like "we regular people" are trying to jump across the Grand Canyon in a single bound - minus our out-to-the-laundry capes and monogrammed spandex jumpsuits.

Perhaps "I think I can!!!" will work here.
IF not, smaller cracks may be the best option.

J. B. Simple(ly) Enlightened

Remembering Langston Hughes...

I went to Harvard, attended Yale and graced the halls of Princeton.
My thoughts were pragmatic; my views accepted; and my ideas
 viewed enlightened.
Fraternities supped in my honor, and footballs touched down in my
 favor.
I was quite the best in all the sports and all the girls were in my
 corner.
And at the end of it all, campaign trophies and tributes in frames
 filled my walls.
They were glassed-in seals, leatherette encased – all testimony to
 my fame.
They gave no hints of race, creed or national origin, just my name.

There were no testaments that informed Onassis, Hughes or Rockefeller
 that I was one of the chosen few – of the one or two that made the
 grade and had the shade of pigmented complexion that waived the
 rules and waved the naps that covered the sink and stopped the drain
 when I washed my hair.
And it wasn't fair.

There were no recommendations and introductions that let them know that
 the tools of my trade had no straws. No letters told them that the
 rundown shacks and slums out back were not my style.
I was used to better.

No statements proclaimed Veteran's Village hand-me-downs and Goodwill
 seconds-round didn't suit my form, and that caviar was on my daily
 menu that pinot chardonnay not muscatel rinsed my mouth.

No footnotes were added for cabbies that would make them
 stop on Lenox to take my fare.
None to police in ghetto situations (PIGS) that would admonish,
 no sticks, no pistols, no cuffs – "Handle with care!"

Continued...

They made no mention of the "Be like the White Man Act" that
 forbids men with B.A.'s, M.A.'s and Ph. D.'s, and Black by no fault
 of their own, from inhabiting jails, riding rails, or hanging like
 'Strange Fruit' by monkeys' tails.

So, what good was all that paper for... To pass some test? To be
 better than the rest? Truly, it is a sad state-of-affairs that my fate
 should hang by a hair, as I hang-out on the corner of 1600
 Pennsylvania, Northwest...

I am not sure of the game that's being played, but the name on my
 diploma is wrong. It isn't right.

Now a self-made man, the name's Simple, not SPADE??!!

Smitten

Forgoing the "wise counsel" of the multitudes
I have decided not to follow a recipe relationship called "normal"
Instead, I will savor every moment of you in my best imaginings...

Our conversations will be flavored with longings and dulcet tones...
Alluding to ancho chili and cayenne ingredients from Caribbean nights
Where our joy lives on sandy knolls, moist beaches for reclining and salty air
Singing melodies full of your name to accompany heart's visions...
I will fantasize until you hold me close enough to still my wandering
hands and lips moving to caress your lobes...

Until then I remain smitten nightly – dialing your number...
To appease an appetite that is addicted and never sate without
The sultry notes surrounding my name from your lips
Preceded by "Baby..." followed by "you are the Love of my life..."

Family...

Thorns, stems and deep roots.
They are connected...and a system for God's garden
A plan that works in total harmony
A colorful family

Without connections to sweet earth
There would be no flowers
No stems to hold 'works of art' aloft
No leaves or petals, no landing pads for sweet honey
 bees.

With no thorns there'd be nothing to inspire second
 thoughts
About tampering with God's perfection
No grassy tabletops, or shade for the season
No meadows for us to see

Together, we are God's best intentions and creations
Sunflowers, black-eyed susans, daffodils and
 dandelions a plenty
But best of all..., like rainbow colors, and rain forest
 Flowers, we are connected. We are a family.
All different but all part of sweet harmony

The perfect picture – a wild meadow surrounding a
 mountain lake
The perfect song – chirping and buzzing and a
 clicking symphony
All connected and meant to be...
We are a family

HE

Yesterday, I saw "him" again.
"Him who?"
"Him the man.

He strode, walked, stepped and laid a path like a surveyor,
through rush hour traffic,
And delayed not once in strides long and sure,
that carried him without incident from
corner to corner to his following.
He was a street corner poet.

His walk was one of impudence unchallenged.
His face was lean and hard.
His eyes were keen, and his brows chiseled stone.

Women hung on his every word, and men shuddered in
personal reproach of themselves and strove for his approval.
He was sought after, looked up to, and well followed - feared
by some, but respected by all..., especially by me.

His finger was a baton that flailed the air,
giving cadence to his syncopated narrations, and rhythm to his
actions.

His body was a sounding board for the bass notes of his voice,
and a well-oiled instrument of creative dance and hip.

I could only guess at what he said, since I heard nothing above the
noise all around.

But he did speak, because his lips moved,
and all who stood around seemed to listen,
and understand.

As he moved, they crowded around and were
like grains of sand, moved by a wave...backward, forward, and often from
side to side;
all in unison in the motion of his tide.

Continued...

He motivated, entranced, and inspired – a
Black Talisman and taskmaster.
Friend to none, he walked alone,
and I longed to walk in his steps.

From a distance I called him "The Man".
At home, I called him "Father".

Paradise Come Full Circle

I was grateful for the darkness that hid my face as we talked
As you placed your words on pulse points with laser precision
I held my breath and listened, fearing my laughter, like a ceramic
    mask at carnival would slip away, to break on the tiles at my feet
Confused and afraid, I turned away lest my sadness be revealed
Replacing fear, I found moments of recent passion and realized
In the fleeting "now," that I had an angel in my grasp and
    struggled to hold on
Trying to suck the juices of joy from her…, as if…
Like the fruit, it would give me true knowledge…, to know her –
    only to realize
My time had passed, and the garden gates were closing as my
    fingers were being pried apart
No longer confused but alone, I turned away lest my view of
    paradise be forever lost…
You called out to me with memories to fuel fires that smoldered
    beneath damp leaves
And pulled me from cynical to hope-filled thoughts of another day
    and night with you
Now renewed and craving the touch that fills a cup, my soul's
    thirst to quench
And I treasure the heart that whispered beautiful lines to a willing
    heart
The words bound for life to lips and arms of an angel that pulled
    me back
No longer lonely, I turned again to reclaim a paradise almost lost,
    now home, now new again…

My mother used to say "The world is full of givers and takers. Which will you be?" This was just one of her favorite sayings to her children. Sometimes I thought her other pithier caveats were probably better suited to conversations among sailors. I don't share those, but I still hear her voice.

Freedom's Dance

There can be no taking for granted the "Freedom Dance"
No forgetting what has brought us to this point and why we now experience a dance revival.
Could it be no water cannons or fire hoses pushing us to the ground – no en masse "waterboarding"
Or perhaps the absence of growling and barking dogs tearing at our clothing
Without delay, dance now for freedom

Could it be the right to love whom we please, or to hold an infant son of color
Or perhaps the absence of glass and razor wire around pipes atop concrete walls to keep "liberty and justice" out
Without delay, usher them into your consciousness and dance now for freedom

Could it be our unshackling and the fact that handcuffs do not crowd our consciousness – no life of fear
Or perhaps my unleashed imagination that dares to put words on bleached fiber for new Ephesians here
Without delay, beatified with grace, power and love - dance now for freedom

Could it be thoughts are now able to reach heights with no glass overhead or entitlement limitations
Or perhaps a baby freed from poison that fills its veins – like leaded wine – a sweet and deadly imitation
Without delay, remember our legacy and dance now for freedom

Could it be trying to figure out how to share a new world with Soweto, Sudan and Syria
Or perhaps it is appreciation that my release is wrapped in history - a gift for which I have paid nothing

Without delay, shake off "satisfied" and dance now for freedom
Could it be that new ears now hear the freedom songs being played across our nation - the world
Or perhaps a call for all to dance for the sake of freedom's memory before the "entitled 1%" can dismantle America

Continued...

Without delay, stand up – arise and dance now for freedom
There can be no taking for granted the "Freedom's Dance"
Her mandate is for steadfast purpose and continued striving as our only chance.

Without delay, grab the hand of a neighbor and begin in unison the "Freedom Dance"

Sweet Dreams...

New coals fuel the smoldering ashes on damp leaves
And pulls me from cynical to hope-filled thoughts
of anticipation and promises of night renewals
and cravings for the touch that fills a cup
My soul's thirst to quench as a telltale heart
delivers rhythmic assurances of life to mine
bound to lips and arms of an angel
To beautiful thoughts and lines of renewal...
It is of your sweetness I dream

Working Out

I fantasize, that our bodies are sounding boards...,
for pleasures – yours and mine?
Trained bodies flexed and trimmed, and breathing deeply
to push up and away and slowly back again.
Biceps to pull on and triceps to push on, and pecs to rest upon.
In pleasure I see your smile, as I sweat, and retreat to the
other side of the bed completed, and you glow from exercises of passion...
For this ultimate moment of ecstasy as one connected by fingertips.
In peace, I think perhaps that sleep is the thing that calls me first...
When I know in fact that it is your breast I crave...
And not rest for my renewal...

Broken

Thinking myself safe, I hid "true nature" and my heart in the darkness of night. While a spotlight in the heavens followed me from place to each new hiding place, I crawled into dark tunnels and wells too deep to fathom – that spewed blackest night to devour light.

Deafening whispers of haunting fears smothered my shouts, as I waited for the reluctant light of day – while despair embraced me like a persistent suitor. Mirrors surrounded me reflecting the inner visions of my anguish showing me "no way out."

Recordings of a childhood gone missing, misplaced wisdom, and yesterday's pain looped continually. To haunting choruses singing, my "dis-ease" and distress harmonizing a dissonant cry. In voids, fear planted dead crops nearer to my heart smothering any "hope" and reinforcing "its lies."

Even as I gripped the handle of a dreaded revolving answer, I dared not name. I uttered a voiceless scream for help - through clenched teeth, replete with shame - a plea for revival. In a place where no way out was the way – I cried out for light and a path to survival. In the most desperate moment, when all seemed lost. Your voice was an audible answer.

A parched heart heard a voice to heal a cancer - salvation and "Living Waters of New Life" - the answer. To push in waves and light the way, as the night receded to disclose a promised redemption from strife. Now, in the truth of day, it is a story of hope – a testimony – a secret oft of men - a rebuke to fear.

No longer hidden from the world's dismay but a lesson for all to share - all that hear. Death now departs in the company of despair and dismay, is replaced with a Light to show the way.

Concentrated Truth Juice...
Condensed sweet milk and strong medicine.

"Madea isn't long for this world," mama used to say.
For years now, despite that pronouncement, she lived on.
She was on borrowed time that God kept lending.
She hung in there when 100 years had come and gone.
She was still here..., on His time – *GPT (God's People's Time)*, and
    the world was blessed with her concentrated truth juice.
"ONLY available here!"

"Madea has seen more than most should," mama would add.
Above her cataracts and bushy white brows was a forehead of
    supple black leather.
Deep wrinkles are disguised by braided wool, imported like
    cotton from fields of the deep South.
Seed planted here grew into robust thoughts that stimulated and
    stymied even great minds.
These furrowed rows were the source of concentrated truth
    juice.
"ONLY available here!"

"Madea says what she knows and doesn't care who witnesses
    her pronouncements," mama warned.
Her observations and knowledge of humanity, or lack
    thereof...could fill volumes.

Her words were always 10 months pregnant with meaning, and
    her eyes underlined, punctuated and engraved.

In her messages, people found shame, reproach..., or a serving of
    concentrated truth juice.
"ONLY available here!"
"Madea really loves her grandbabies," mama proclaimed.
She always had hugs, a spare knee, or knees, and arms that could carry us,
    enfold or hold us just right.

She smelled of sweetness, vanilla and cookies, and things she created only for
    her *babies*.

Continued...

Her love for us was like the condensed sweet milk she used to make hot chocolate.
And it was "ONLY available here!"

"Madea was like concentrated truth juice when she lived here," I now tell my children.
"You might not want to drink her message down full-strength."
"She should have had a warning label on her," we'd laugh.

WARNING! Dilute Before Consuming!
Madea's truth is **Strong Medicine**!"
"ONLY available here!"

My words try to be like the condensed milk Madea used for sweet rolls.
Someday, I will hold my babies close and make hot cocoa, when I share her stories.
Waking up with their heads on my lap will be memories for their lifetime.
One day, they will tell their children of me, Madea and concentrated truth juice.
"ONLY available here!"

Reflection on Truth Juice

My mother used to say "The world is full of givers and takers. Which will you be?" This was just one of her favorite sayings to her children. Sometimes I thought her other pithier caveats were probably better suited to conversations among sailors. I don't share those, but I still hear her voice.

I laugh now at my sensibilities and her insight. She's probably laughing today from heaven, where she, Matthew, Mark, Luke, or John look down and watch as I share the same warnings with my children.

Now I say things like, "Most people that call you *friend* are only *acquaintances*. Know the difference!" Madea was the original Afro-American Truth Juice.

Her observations of fact were concentrated to the point of being solid – more like bricks. Her quick wit and retorts were legendary. She would strap the truth to the end of an arrow and take aim. Watch out! It wouldn't be pretty or pleasant, but it was always appropriate to the moment – on target, on time and honest. Not because she was "speaking her truth" but because she was on point for protecting someone not able to do it for themselves.

I laugh now and pass her words on to my children. I have now become my mother. Smiles.

My Plans in His Time...New Normal

My sister Rita describes a phenomenon called *"New Normal."*

New Normal is dictated by a process of praying for direction and guidance; going with what you know; hoping for His best; and adjusting your plan when He repeats His for the hard of hearing.

With new normal, her vision is now considerably closer. His wisdom has shortened her arms and she is now near sighted. The long-view – tomorrow, is out of sight and at best, a hoped-for evolution.

So today with new normal, she stands beside her son who battles his cancerous enemy – one moment at a time. Now, with her sights adjusted to the end of her nose and aides to hearing Him firmly in place, she considers today a gift and a grace-filled answer to her simple prayer.

"Give me peace, Lord."

Don't Wanna Be No Accident...

Pass the suntan lotion, sunblock (now) and the "Invisible Man."

This high-yella Brother is heading over to the tanning booth...
You can laugh all you want, but I ain't gonna be nobody's accident, or statistic.
I dealt with that stuff in the "60's" when my alligator platforms, and my coolness let the revolutionaries know I was no snake.
But, my walk ain't cool now, and saggin' my pants around my knees has got no class.
It just shows parts of my sunburned anatomy that I used to call my...
Assuming I had time to be heard, I could sound like Eldridge, or Huey.
But I may not get the time to talk, so you'd recognize the radical me.
Or even the Denzel walk. My tan will have to say it all.
"I am the tall, Brown and slightly burnt Brutha on the walker.
So, pass the suntan lotion – SPF 200, the Invisible Man, and The Man Who Cried I Am.
Hey, step back..., close that can.
It's me!"

The Revolutionary's Manifesto

The hot and latter days of the revolution were not "Cool."
But, "We, the people" were standing for something as "united we stood…" our fists raised meant we knew what that something was.
"Lift every voice and sing, 'till earth and heaven ring."

We had a message with meaning recited and repeated with meaning by Maya, Malcolm and Martin, Huey and Eldridge, or people of color as bright as the morning and as black as the night…We sang,
"Ring with the harmonies of Liberty; let our rejoicing rise high as the listening skies."

Sometimes, it sounded angry.
We called for righteousness and indignation when Lewis Allan's words were penned - a lilting poem, to sing as a song up north, as *strange fruit* still hung rotting on trees in the not so distant south…Still we chanted…,
"Sing a song full of the faith that the dark past has taught us. Sing a song full of the hope that the present has brought us."

The message was almost forgotten.
The enemy's face was so distorted that we no longer recognized it, and mistakenly killed one brother and then another because the song's meaning was faded. So now, we are Déjà vu'ing at a revolution that stands for something. After finally arriving, it looks like the beginning again. So, "Facing the rising sun of our new day begun, let us march on 'til victory is won…"

So now we sing lest we forget…
"Let us march on 'til victory is won…"

Dark Night of the Soul...

I've been in tunnels dark and wells too deep to fathom...
Sounds around, deafened me with whispers of my fears.
And when light finally made its way to me...years had passed.
Mirrors surrounded me reflecting the inner visions of my anguish...
Recordings of my childhood, my manhood, and all my yesterdays looped continually.
The haunting voices of a ghostly chorus sang my pain and repeated in dissonance – "Hopeless!"
My fear replanted a dead crop nearer to my heart to smother any chance of recovery.
I screamed for help through clenched teeth and fists and cried out for revival.
In my most desperate moment, when no ear could hear me, You answered my cry.
You spoke my name for salvation – my heart heard your voice and embraced a new life.
The night has now ended, and the promise of "Life" is bright and irrevocable.

Liberation Day

"Trapped within a body with a life sentence."

Now well past youth
I am trapped within a movin',
Shrinkin' prison
with no out...no release.
With failin' communication -
words garbled and ciphered.
No tellin' how long this sentence's gonna last.

It was pleasant at first.... invincible
Smooth walls - streamlined shapes,
but cracks are now appearing
where once was none,
and the plumbing's shot to hell
with no out – no release.
No tellin' how long this sentence's gonna last.

It's gettin' musty in here.
The ventilation is gettin' worse,
and the lights are startin' to fail
in this slower movin' mobile jail.
Smotherin' my shouts for release,
but no out and no relief.
Ain't no tellin' how long this sentence's gonna last.

It's shrinkin' day by day,
Sluggish jerkin' - once smooth motions.
There's been a sudden stop...
My jail don't move, and my cell's gone silent.
The air has stopped circulatin'.
And now, the door is gone.

Today is Liberation Day.
I am free.

Exhaustible

SOMETIMES I find myself hovering between sleep and waking, as I press the button repeatedly to tarry in this place where my reality is no dream – where there are no limits to my passions or my brilliance, and I am in no rush to reach the goal. And the journey is far too important to rush, as I consciously push immeasurable between seconds.

SOMETIMES, I feel certain there is **NO END** to time and **FOREVER** is conceivable. And **ONLY** tomorrow will provide all the opportunities promised by life today and more...
IF I am right, there is no reason to rush even though I am anxious for an even better day.
So, waiting for tomorrow is a good reason to do **NOTHING** until then, because there is more than enough time for **EVERYTHING**.

SOMETIMES I **KNOW** that **SOMEDAY** my understanding will exceed my ability to question. AND **ON THAT** tomorrow, I will awaken smarter than the night before..., and I will discover that just **MAYBE** genius will be a function of hanging out and **NOT** hanging on. Just **MAYBE** there will still be a chance of making the same mistakes **AGAIN** with positive consequences.

SOMETIMES, I know that passions are forever..., and **ONLY** some distant tomorrow will provide enough time to eclipse the joy of today..., **WHEN** our heavenly bodies collided again and again..., mimicking the birth of dwarf stars, and we calculate infinite as the depth of after-glow..., and count eternity repeating this time of love.

SOMETIMES I think, maybe the noise blaring for my attention **is JUST A DREAM**, and a power outage out there could leave me in the arms of a lover - pushing eternity between waiting seconds... or drag reluctant hours between minutes to keep a sunset in view as wings lift me beyond the clouds...

SOMETIMES I HOPE, JUST MAYBE, there will be no need to reach out for that distant place that signals the end of peace and quiet – as I finally lie down in a meadow or fall into the arms of rest – I contemplate numbers through bleary eyes. And **JUST MAYBE I** am pushing at some temporal button for just a while by creating a concept called "Eternity"

My Love Won't Wait...

In our times, you've waxed warm and cold
I'm never sure which way to go.
Uncertainty has tainted our time, for someone else holds your
    mind.
Not knowing what to do, I've sung you love songs to melt your
    heart, and written lines so you'd know that...
Knowing you has bewitched and beguiled me.
And for my time your love has made me whole.
But my love won't wait forever.

I've waited on your touch for so many years.
Crying silently when no one saw the tears,
I dreamed that I would someday hold your hand as more than just
    a friend.
Not knowing what to do, I've sung you love songs to melt your
    heart, and written lines so you'd know that...
Knowing you has bewitched and beguiled me
And for my time your love has made me whole.
But my love won't wait forever.

Now the decision is all but made.
Your heart has again gone home.
Being near enough to touch, but never close enough to hold you,
gives new meaning to my pain.

The pain won't let me stay and I hope you understand that what
    I've had to say has never been more true.
There is solitude but no distance between us for you are in my
    soul.

Not knowing what to do, I've sung you love songs to melt your
    heart, and written lines so you'd know *that*...
Knowing you has bewitched and beguiled me and for my time your
    love has made me whole.
But my love won't wait.

"Picture Perfect" ...

I'll know "Picture Perfect" when my window frames it
A vision of fall colors resting on spring dresses
And autumn coats of tweed... Yes, indeed

I'll know "Picture Perfect" when color-filled hues and shadows of gray
Drape faces, shoulders and hands at work and play – just out of reach
Passing unaware outside my shop in search of an afternoon coffee stop

I'll know "Picture Perfect" when our best – somewhere deep within longs to be out
When strollers and families languish 'neath streetlights at dusk - day's end
With snow-cones, friendly feelings, gelato and trust

I'll know "Picture Perfect" as the gesso of winter white wipes away traces
Of imperfection, however improbable and good times long to reappear, when
Goodwill and love no longer away...Now, are back at home to stay

I'll know "Picture Perfect" as I pray troubled seasons end – as
Joy and peace are new and perfect pictures – our wounds to mend
On plywood compositions - weapons of love and peace - not munitions

I'll know "Picture Perfect" in times of renewed humanity
Now growth – new love in all season – now a time of family
Now perfect again when tears ending – a blue moon, rainbow
colors and love in bloom

I'll know "Picture Perfect" when my window once more frames a perfect you
When you arrive and I am here ... waiting too
We're home again – so different, but now alike - not a twin
I'll know "Picture Perfect" when we stand face to face
Hand to outstretched hand, determined to find a place

Common ground for lives that matter for one and all
proud and tall...all together

I'll know "Picture Perfect" when community, family and I are connected as One
Just a perfect 20/20 vision..., when we find ways of healing – a perfect way
to begin
Just a Perfect picture when all my windows and doors,
are portals to light again

I'll know "Picture Perfect" then...

In the twinkle of an eye...

In the twinkle of an eye, a lifetime has worn my rough to smooth, and all my yesterdays have evaporated.

Wasn't it just yesterday when the first lingering touches of passion pulled us from the arms of youth to parenthood?

Didn't we hold onto every dance when I pressed a breathless you against me and held you against uncertain steps, to put off the time when curfew would call you home?

A blink later, didn't I steal a first kiss on your front porch, and repeatedly in hallways, stairways and pathways we traveled – through the years?

Wasn't it only just yesterday, 40 years and one tear later when we kissed to fan embers that **faded** – but never our love?

Now I know that I've lived my life in short minutes and in each moment found a reason for being here – your love.

In the twinkle of an eye, a lifetime has slipped away and left its traces – barely tangible remnants of today – at twilight, fading away. Wasn't it just today when I beheld the wonders of nature?

When Spring awaking, roused sleeping bouquets of daffodils, and peonies a plenty...? And suddenly God orchestrated unique floral arrangements out of basins of mud and brown grass.

And then nightly, didn't the stars fall into graduated blackness at the ocean's edge – at the end of view – to find a home in the ocean deep, or in the puddled reflection at my feet.

Today, in my old age, didn't I witness a miracle when a cowgirl in tight jeans – that looked so much like you, crossed the street in rush hour to stop traffic and time? Forever, I held a breath between in and out and remembered you.

I've lived my life in short minutes and in each moment found a reason for being here – your love.

Continued...

In the twinkle of an eye, a lifetime has melted to no time at all, and tomorrow has gone missing.

Will it be tomorrow, when I spy a monarch perched atop the tallest blade of grass, as it pushes winds with massive wings... and billowed sails halfway around the world?

Won't a whippoorwill's melody in the darkness sing out to night creatures in need of accompaniment and bring me God's harmony?

In a twinkle of an eye, I am certain that tomorrow is gone. For now, the finish line is beneath my feet. In what seems a moment to me, I have started, run the race and finished first - with no preparation or training.

Now I know that, "I've seen God's wonders, and had my share of fleeting glances – my misplaced chances. Isn't life grand, and gone like a flash?"

I've lived my life in short moments of eternity and in each moment found a reason for being here – the love we shared.

(Blackened) Rose...

    I do remember a blackened rose that wasn't always so...
    It is wilted but alive in my memories ...

    Its life began with the promise of being a blossom –
    a symbol of you and our love.
    Its smell vowed to linger in my mind like the fresh
    perfume of passion on wrinkled linen ...
    Its deep red blush was reminiscent of our heat and
    the vitality of our relationship.
    But nothing lasts forever, and even this blossom has
    faded – leaving behind the memory of one perfect
    day.

    Today there is only a blackened rose that wasn't
    always so..., and less than perfect recollections that
    promised to stay.

One Degree of Separation...

A Delicious apple from a single tree in the orchard transplanted half the world away is still a Delicious apple. The beauty of this model is that the sweetness of the fruit remains the same and is not diminished by distance.

The new orchard from this apple is connected by more than genetics, or distant roots – energy and spirit are boundless.

In life, we share ideas that do not lose their brilliance or sweetness with repeated telling.
As family, we are not limited by location, but remain part of the whole. The sweetness of relationship is not diminished, 'though separated by continents.

The new family and old are connected by more than genetics – the threads on the loom are the history, the stories and the words we bring with us.

"How sweet it is..." Look to the miracle of orchards for family ties, and the one degree of separation that makes us all family.

Once a Home

Home is where we once escaped to be alone, to embrace and to see our reflection in love-struck eyes. But now, empty rooms with dusty remains and dried tears bid us farewell. And Nancy Wilson singing 'A House is Not a Home', is a love song's echo of days long gone – a reminder of pain, and broken dreams in search of healing.

Flowers Don't Fly

Flowers don't fly, my love.
They only provide a hiding place for butterflies,
Who paint the skies, give color to air, and hide in
berets of your hair - the petals of the most beautiful
flower I know.

Home in the Deep

When was the last time you saw a dolphin in a pond?
A puddle on the sidewalk is no place for whales.
In the ocean - your heart is where deep things reside.
Why couldn't I be a creature at home in shallow and less
complicated places, or just an angel fish in your bowl?

Leaving' Love Behind

I stood on the corner
waiting for you to have
a change of heart
that never came
and neither did you.

One Perfect Rose...

I see distant meadows...

On a day much like today I followed a bee.
In a rolling meadow, I watched intently to see,
a sight for once, meant only for me.

He stopped here..., there and finally away
not delaying, but clear in purpose for his season.
Out of breath and running, I spied the reason.

In this field of daffodils and 'mums aplenty...
many with nectar and colored dew...
Stood a single perfect rose that looked like you.

Her stem was supple, and petals were of braided silk...
She waited in clear view with innocence her duty,
Poised like no other as if to hide her beauty...

A gentle breeze with minor corrections called and
carried the bee... to waiting petals that offered a home...
and for this moment in time seemed an elegant throne.

Like no other, she was not for the picking, ...
She was a unicorn among zebras...
A diamond among coal..., platinum among gold.

He stayed for a while and maybe for life...
What a perfect union – a bee, a rose – his wife...

But then came dusk and then the night and I will never know
how one perfect rose came to be in this distant meadow.

'Twas on that single day I came to see...
A relationship in the making for one searching bee.

In a distant meadow, often in clear view...
Just beyond the door, stands a perfect rose – that would
be you and the happy bee would be me.

All That Matters

Love is what's left, when looks don't mean much anymore, but I proudly hold the hand of my **plump wrinkled beauty**.
Love is what's left when **independence is replaced by helplessness**, and the one who **feeds and freshens me** finds joy in caring for every need.

Love is what I found in the garden when
I watched you sparing worms while cultivating hyacinths, tulips and 'mums.
Love is what even unflattering body parts arouse when I think of the aged beauty they belonged to, and how I once held you near.

It's what's left...the best of all there ever was in my life and the best of me to you ...
It's ALL that's left worth cherishing...and what I remember even though you're gone...
Love is what's in the eyes when the last hours won't provide breath to whisper or the strength to utter.

And when I leave to join you, this page will be a legacy left to tell our children...
That Love is what's left behind.
Love to live on, and to live for...
It's the best of what's left and all that really mattered, anyway.

Every Morning...

I miss you.

When I woke this morning, the stillness told me what I knew. I reached out and the impression you'd left had already forgotten you... No longer warm, the bed held only a wrinkled memory in sheets you once caressed. My heart and salt on my pillow, reminded me that you were no dream. 'Though I couldn't see you going, the distance between us was growing.
I knew immediately that emptiness had returned and today you would not.

When I woke this morning the smell of you lingered in the air like memories of your kisses. Feelings of loss were the alarm that woke me, and my anguish summoned old fears. Screams echoed in my soul and your name ran to comfort the hurt in my chest, accompanied by shame. 'Though I didn't hear you going, the distance between us was growing.
I knew immediately that loneliness had returned and today you could not.

When I woke this morning, my marrow knew the chill of alone. The heat of your body once signaled your presence and warmed me. Blankets pulled to recover it, felt hollow, empty, and left a vacuum for your return. 'Though I couldn't stop you from going and the distance between us was growing. I knew immediately that solitude was returning and today you could not.

When all the tomorrows wake me, only memories will greet me. I'll know that more than just recently you've been away. I'll wonder how long I've been feeling lonely and alone, and from the kitchen, I'll see a bed our love no longer owns. 'Though I won't stop remembering, as the distance between us is growing, I'll know again, that emptiness has returned, and you will not. ·

Continued...

Each morning I wake, I'll remember you leaving again –
not quite so desperate as the morning before. I'll pray it's
your movements that I hear – that it's you walking
through darkness to embrace me, as I lay quietly,
pretending not to have noticed that you've gone and
returned. And at your first touch, my hunger for you will
quicken to welcome you home. But even then, I will know
that when night departs, so will you.

On some tomorrow morning when all hope is gone,
you will wake. Your memories will reach out to touch
the hollow beneath your breasts I once filled. The
warmth in a space and in empty places will escape,
and even though I couldn't see me going, I haven't
been given a choice. You'll miss me and know I've
gone to places you cannot. On that "Tomorrow," I
will change the lock on my heart, and we will know
that emptiness has claimed a space that you have
not.

Exits

Exits are not my forte . . .

I never know...

I never really know when you'll smile sweetly, easing
my retreat to the door, or give hell to the head you
held gently... just a moment before.
I never really know when the time, or the feelings
will be right to say, *"Goodbye for now."*

So, I wait 'til your easy breathing on smoldering
embers signals the time for me to slip quietly from
the sheets and your embrace.
I will steal silently through darkened rooms...,
to pause briefly at the door to listen for your sighs,
and to leave behind an angel kiss.

And with no witness to watch my Dis-Ease,
the light of day will tell you that...
Exits are not my forte.

Still

In rough times, I smiled when I thought of you.
At leisure and daydreaming, you inhabited my thoughts.

When work was frantic, with no time to think...
I'd break the rules and smile about you and me.
When the days were done, I'd rush home to your waiting arms.
Our lips' first touch would ignite my hunger and my lips smiled
    knowing that our kisses were missing each other.

In the dark when we made love, I smiled the most
    knowing that I was the lucky one who would
    witness the fireworks filling my heaven with
    only you...

Now, as I sit alone facing the fireplace, the embers speak to me.
The logs wait to ignite and remind me of years in between, when
    I too burned hot.
As I remember, I chuckle quietly to myself and wink at your
    picture.

I suspect you are smiling, too.
When I smile, I think of you, yet and...**still**.

Pinholes in Fabric

I know that understanding "my life and its meaning" are gifts received in due time. They are like islands connected to continents, but in ways hidden from view. Like grains of sand when near enough to see, and like deserts from afar.

In my time, they are chapters in a history where I am the main character, but in eternity they are surely periods and marks at the end of this sentence, or maybe just fly specks in the paper. I'd hope for more – even a single letter on the Library of Congress shelves.

In the search to "be" and understand, fickle views through pinholes in fabric sometimes tease out clues to my identity. I daydream and imagine, and finally exhort and pray for a revelation. Eventually, I find that the understanding is in the final punctuation – retrospect and seeing my world after shapes and informs me...

I see through my pinhole, that friends are not the ones who agree with everything I do, but they make the decision to love me none-the-less and evermore.

Through my pinhole, I tally the treasures of my love as the measures of my willingness to lay down my life for you – "...no greater love."

Through my pinhole, I understand that my children are not the products of my loins, but the evolution of a greater plan.

Through my pinhole, I see that today isn't a promise kept, and tomorrow REALLY won't be assured, not even to me.

Through my pinhole, I try to understand God's plan by looking at the universe through a single telescope – like contemplating a single grain of sand from space.

Through my pinhole, I see what is invisible except eyes-full, one night at a time – when starry lights gratefully lift a cirrus curtain on a blackened stage to amaze me.

Continued...

I suspect that I am viewing the parts of God that I will never understand, but SHe sees and knows all of me.

So, inspecting the picture of "Who" and "What" I really am, may only be through a pinhole at an appointed time just for me. With perfectly imperfect vision, I see a life that was meant to be and simply smile. It is relative…

After all, a "3" looks like an "E" upside down, and only SHe knows how I should be seeing it. And isn't "8" really infinity on end? These are the limits to my simple understanding that I never realized before.

A "?" or a period makes all the difference, but only at the end. So, I will be patient to get to the goal, since rushing is not an option in God's timing. And perfected view won't happen on this plane.

And SHe did shake the bag that created the watch. I doubt SHe ever expected me to take the time to repeat the miracle in my time.

So with the little that I've seen through my pinhole, I just sigh and whisper "Amazing!"

There were Black Cowboys...?

There were Black Cowboys, weren't there?

Today, they bussed me to a school where people looked at me as if I was alien.
Garbage was suddenly perfume. I was much less and not so sweet.
My hand raised for questions, closed to a fist that became my constant companion that I buried at my side.
And, my question went unanswered.

There were Black Cowboys, weren't there?

Yesterday was a first, and today will not be the last.
My determination grew during the night and somehow, I rose knowing I'd make it through the day.
Yesterday were barbs and insults, but today not even recognition.
I came with an open mind, but nothing constructive is in the air to fill it.
Maybe tomorrow will be better.

There were Black Cowboys, weren't there?

Today, as the final bell rang, rocks pitted the outer skin of the bus.
Rotten tomatoes hurt my feelings and bruised my pride as I sat on the big bus...all banana yellow, surrounded by pained faces as we fled away. So I determined, tomorrow I'd work harder to find an answer to my question.

There were Black Cowboys, weren't there?

After yesterday, we have a new driver who is more apprehensive than the last, but no more than me. And as I got off the bus, there was new tension in the air, and I dared not go inside.
The sea of faces at the door parted to let me pass. But today is stranger than before. Thinking my determination enough for one step at a time, but my tears won't let me stay – not today.
The bus not yet departed, seems a refuge and a safe haven of immense warmth and is eager to spirit me home.
In my guilt for not being courageous, I cry hoping momma won't be too disappointed that I have returned without my answer.

Maybe tomorrow, or next week I'll find it in a place without fear.
There were Black Cowboys, weren't there?

This should have been page 1...

Since it came first ...

But then life isn't always about proper sequence...

Sometimes the best things come in the autumn of life when we have the wisdom to enjoy them, but not the endurance to exhaust them, to explore them, or to conquer them.

We can only look on and look back and smile about what might have been.

We know that the memories shaping our wrinkles will die silently in our breast when we are laid to rest.

Over the years, I've prayed fervently for time travel so that I could send the message back before it was too late.

But since technology has failed me, I now hope for the best. Perhaps a curve in the road "PAST" will *brake* my speed so my eyes will focus enough to read the signs and avoid "TRAVAIL."

"Pay attention, there's a message here!"

This really should have been page one...

The LAST PAGE

Life is so ironic and cruel..., when
Four score and ten is needed to understand what ***IT'S*** all about, and in a flash we're gone. There's no time to pass on the knowledge, or even a warning.

The speed of it all is magnified by a lack of experience. It seems in retrospect that life truly is wasted on the young and inexperienced who don't have the patience to read these lines, or the wisdom to understand their meaning.

Clearly, this was written for the "me" of 40 years ago – too young to understand and rushing into the unknown.

So, looking to a future that's looking to the past... IF time travel has been perfected in my future, and I am reading this before 2060, "Please put this poem on page 2, or at least near the front of the book – after page 1."

What book? Be patient. You'll find out.

(**NOTE:** Read *Page 1* first.)

A Whistle-Stop

> Our passions seem to be
> whistle stops -
> spots in our lives
> we've chosen to share.
> They are times for refueling
> renewing and *getting off*
> *and on* one another – never
> staying long enough
> to see where it's all going,
> or what the trip's about -
> departing after a brief respite
> just as empty as before
> and feeling short-changed
> as we turn off the lights.
>
> For all it might have been,
> Love is not a whistle stop
> or a time for getting off.
> Step forward or stand back.
> The doors are closing.
> Get off, or come in...

by Ronald Montgomery

Surprise me...
Put a flower in your hair.
And I will put you both on a pedestal and
Tell the world about a beauteous bouquet
Of two special blossoms.

Lesson 8 – Opening my Door

Taking chances sometimes means being courageous …
Taking chances sometimes means being courageous … DARE!

Out of fear, **I dare** not open doors to the unknown.
Striving to overcome a fear that desires are too
distant – only to find the distant meadow – a sweet
expectation that I have envisioned, is just beyond
three padlocks and a deadbolt – on the other side of
the door and pushing against my threshold.

Now knowing that fear IS of NOT finding perfection and
strength within myself, in clear view of a world looking on…
But then, life and God's best may be hiding in clear view –
within arms-reach and closer than my planning portends.
The "unlikely" IS possible if I now dare to open the
door and take flight into the meadow. Life really is
about daring to be courageous and **enduring**.

Taking chances sometimes means being courageous …
Taking chances sometimes means being courageous … DARE!

Memories of the Garden

Today I picked a dandelion.
Tomorrow, a tulip will tickle my fancy.
Sometime soon, when I am wiser,
I'll reach out for you and the day after,
My days as a gardener will end.

Surprise me…
Put a flower in your hair.
And I will put you both on a pedestal and
Tell the world about a beauteous bouquet
Of two special blossoms.

Then other flowers will be safe from plucking hands and
My tools will hang rusting in the shed.

Just Breathe...
The Promise

Your quiet sighs and night-time breathing are monuments to the love we share.
They whisper to me of all the reasons I stay.

I hold my breath to hear, in the darkness, an unguarded you that pushes against me now and again to fill the hollows of my stomach and thigh...

As you slide into my embrace – that protects you from the outside..., moans escape with nowhere to go but my waiting ears.
There..., they remain captive memories of love we've shared.

Hearing you is a clear reminder of why I've stayed so long.

Breathe for me and I will keep my promise to stay by your side.
I am listening.

Just breathe.

... a Message

Everybody's got a story. Some have much more.
They have a message. And some have a song to sing.

Everybody's got a song to sing, but some songs are much more. They have a message in their music. The voices still ring in my ears.

Everybody's got a voice to sing their story. And some stories are so much more. The story is much more.
It's a message.

I am the song. You are my story.
The message is love.
Should we sing together?

Tree Feathers in Our Forest Bed

I will crawl beneath the sheets that hold your scent
And dream of sweet dalliances in forests of fall
Our repose covered with orange, brown and violet tree feathers...

Between the leaves...

You will disappear beneath its blanket...
Sought by my touch...found by your heat...our release...
Sounds of the wild, a new song for the forest

Between leaves and blades of grass...

The sweet perfume of your breath on my cheek
My sighs in your ear, I will hide with you beside rocky creeks
And dream of sweet surrender beneath trees so tall

Beneath shadows of a full moon...

For sweet repose...my hands, your lips, my nose
As one...we move, our legs entwined
I will wind among...silken branches

Between the arms of a dream...

For Sweet Repose...the one you chose...
To dream of sweet dalliances in forests of fall
Our bodies entwined as one...
Good Night

Really

My love, and your lack of experience, is no excuse
for misspelling lust - passion and pleasure with no
intention of endurance or building anything that
looks like a relationship.

I am NOT a member of the "NOW" generation that
believes this is all there is – is RIGHT *NOW* with no

consequences, or pretenses of anything more
important than "ME" and the next CLIMAX!

Pushing sheets and pillows into rumpled masses on mattress
pads is not *Love – not in* the '70's, 80's and definitely not
yesterday at Motel 6, 7 or 8.
And definitely not because you could grunt the word.

Get a clue or a dictionary.
If you can't find either, get a VW bus, paisley ties,
flower appliques and a trip back in time.
There is a difference.

I was high back then, but today I know the difference
and recognize deceit.
So, what have I learned, REALLY?
Real Love doesn't come easy, and it's not free.

So, come home.
I will blame your lack of experience and my lack of
understanding.
You are forgiven this time…, REALLY!

Sweet Chocolate

Sometimes I wonder why God has given me so many
Sisters. They are all special and all so very different.
Some seem to be female reflections of me and some
from another planet, but "all my Sistahs." Some days
I think this should be the name of a new soap opera,
and I smile.

God has filled my world with a beautiful spice rack
that I call my family and filled my freezer with
Godiva Chocolates – both light and dark – all my
sisters.

Thank you, God.

Warm Weather Report…Click Click

Some wait anxiously for a morning's weather report to forecast the day's goodness and agonies, and the ups and downs of celestial bodies. But I wait only for your early morning smile to signal the start of sunny interludes 'til you signal the moon to bring out black curtains sprinkled with stars for me to count.

The photo albums on the coffee table and in my mind capture each time you have smiled during our times together.
This is my Farmer's Almanac.
The last page is blank - awaiting the next forecast of your laughter and love.

Today is another opportunity for sunshine and hot winds - your smile and kisses on my forehead with a southerly movement to my lips.
Tomorrow's weather will be more of the same.

Dew and moisture will appear on red petals with expectations of high-pressure heated embraces as we move from the foyer to dark warm places for private, extended showings of the Aurora Borealis and exploding stars.

When the celestial show is complete, you will smile.
Click, click. The shutter will close and
I will add a new page – a blank sheet awaiting the next forecast of your laughter and love.

Full...

On my best days, I've been *full of myself*.
These are the days when I am sure that I have all the right answers. I imagine that I could see it ALL and understand it too, if given the chance.

But, with just half-a-chance, I find I am **OVERWHELMED** with miniscule *knowledge*!
I find myself spinning like a dervish and wondering what I missed to be so off-base.

So **NOW** I settle for 'pinhole' understanding that I've been given, and happily assert that this gift will be enough for my slice of eternity here.

In my new and perfected life, heaven will be my new home, and the stars will be my playground. SHe will give me more understanding than I can even imagine.

So, for **NOW**, *Pinhole Understanding* will be more than enough, and I am covering the other eye to keep from getting confused.

Love WINS...

I've put the scales on level ground to set the balance of what you mean to Me.
In times not so good, you've been attentive, and praised Me for all I was and will always be.
In good times, you've forgotten I even exist as you run from success to success to collect accolades.
Your pleasures moved to distant places and far from Me, and it seems I was unnecessary and better left behind.
Sometimes it seemed that My name was foreign to your tongue and would never again cross your lips.
Missing me and feeling separation in our relationship appeared the farthest thing from your heart.
So now, with all in the scales, you must decide what it all means for you. I know the answer.
With life **centered on you** to the left, and
My love to the right, what will it be?

There is only one answer – Love WINS!

When blessings poured down, and your cup was full to overflowing, you embraced and held Me close.
You praised Me and forgot Me until the endless night of the soul tried to smother your cries for help.
I heard your cries and reached into a darkness blacker than any night to light your way and shelter you from harm.
Again, you held Me as if nothing would ever separate us and I was glad. But now, you have found other solace and happiness in your world without Me. I am saddened and miss you deeply. Without you, it's not the same.
So now, with all in the scales, you must decide what it is telling you, for I know the answer.
With your life *filled with the world* to the left, and
My love to the right, what will it be?

Yesterday, today and tomorrow there is still only one answer – **Love WINS!**

In the morning, midday and midnight when you felt secure and didn't know why, I loved you.

Continued...

I kept you safe within My heart, beneath My gaze and surrounded you with My angels.
When you sank beneath a burden, I lifted the weight, because of a love you didn't understand.
When you ran - from fear of commitment, with a strong desire to be free, I didn't stop you.
I released you and honored free will out of love for you - with no desire to imprison you.
When all has been said, and all has been done, the balance will tell a story.
So now, with all in the scales, your history will tell you the answer I know.

Left is a life ***filled with freedom and out of view***, and ***My LOVE*** is to the right, what will it be?

In the end, as in the beginning, there is but one answer – for your sake **I SAY THAT LOVE WINS!**

Sisters...

You make me smile...

> What are Sisters for, if not to tickle their brothers, and
> To be practical jokers with no regard for retribution
> Knowing that I can't disinherit you, or erase your memory
> Knowing that I feel your pain and sometimes think no Siamese twin could be closer
> Knowing that maybe not today, but someday soon
> I'll find a way to tickle you back, with no mercy
>
> What are Sisters for, if not to show up unexpectedly
> To tell some silly story, that no one but me would laugh at
> Whose antics are without rhyme or reason..., just because
> Whose laughter is contagious and has no antidote

Whose words I'll remember in times not so
    laughable
When I sit in the dark and wonder why God had
    brought me this far...

What are Sisters for, if not to give big brothers a
    hug, and
To say, "I love you for no apparent reason..., or no
    reason at all"
I'll look at things you held, and they will be
    precious to me
I'll think of things you've done, and they will all be
    understandable
I'll think of your silliness and warmth, and know
    that you've made me whole
Not in the past, but in my ever-present memory
    that you inhabit

What's a Sister for, if not to be
The bubbles under my nose when drinking
    champagne
The midday rain through sunlight that never hides
The sand between my toes escaping ocean waves
What are Sisters for, if not to create memories

I remember all of my Sisters and count myself
    blessed

Heroes Got no Guarantee of Tomorrow

(Heroes need theme music too.)

Hugh Masekela's bright sounds blast from
the past on WGNU... "Da... da...da..DAH...DAH" ...
(Soulful Struts plays in the background)

Unbeknownst to most, we've been heroes all along.
Not always singing with the rest...
but humming a special song...
to the sounds of steel bands, and drums,
calypso, and jazz, and trumpets blaring es-specially for "US."
The messages clear, are embedded in special
songs that speak of feelings and
written in "Mumbo-Jumbo" –
embroidered and woven
not into brocade, velvets or silks, but into kente cloth.
One strand at a time, making daily changes...
Not a "Future Dream," but a special "Present."
We speak of culture here...
"Pass it on!"
(Curtis rumbles "Do you share with Black Folks not of kin...?")

A dream to pass on...
The conviction, values and pride fueled by lines
of (Richard) Wright, (Langston) Hughes – our
J. B. Simple in countless rhymes...;
all weavers of the cloth.
Heroes need poetry and theme music, ...
revolution's songs of hope.
One friend at a time and one lifetime
is our promise kept...
We speak of character and strength...
"Pass it on!"

A hero's work... plain, stands like a tree...
Sturdy cowboys, lofty pilots,
scientist and plumbers,
masons and kings...the song ripples on.
Their words and deeds leave a mark.
But even the hearts of heroes skip a beat...

Continued...

Tomorrow's not guaranteed...,
one promise
at a time to keep.
Share the dream in my time...
"Pass it on!"

We speak of love here.

"Pass it on to tomorrow's heroes!
Pass it on. Pass it on!
Patti refrains, "When you are blessed pass it on"

No Simple Promise

Deep within my chest
A single breath fills my lungs to bursting
As I sigh, grateful for the preciousness of life
And listening intently to a place
Where life's nectar feeds me
I hear a single beat – yet another
Repeated to remind me
That promises are not meant to be broken
But no breath or beat is promised
Each is delivered as a gift

Happy Birthday

With eyes opening, the celebration begins again
I will know that "Life" is presence
And presents of love
A promise given and kept
Again, again and again
With each new tomorrow
Thank you

Unspoken...

History Lessons

You give feeling and color to words that otherwise
serve only as the mechanics of **"talk"** and **"write"**
as I sit at your side listening to field-lore, family stories,
and passed on fables where you were the main character,
the main observer, or just the main perpetrator of....

I hear anew, stories retold on occasions –
too numerous to count, as you unlock my soul
and give me hope that in my tomorrows,
"Once upon a time" will also be a series of short preambles
describing a better time "When, we used to..."
Or, when youth was a series of moments in time -
followed by **another** and **yet another** – all
connected in some unseen way to ..."It seems like just yesterday..."

I use your unspoken words, now that you're gone, heated by my
singularly heady passion in my "Nows."
I spice tomorrow's languid evenings with life's
seasoned appreciation...handed down by you, and recount to my
grandsons and granddaughters your field-lore, family stories, ...
and even the fables where I was the main character, the main
observer or just the main perpetrator of the most unbelievable
antics...
It **WILL BE** a vicarious vision, retold on the porch, and to be passed
on to my children's children...

"Once upon a time..., when we used to... in Saint Louis.
And it **seems like just yesterday**...," when "**Grandma Ruby**" told
this story to me, so I could tell it to you...

Stories for Hot Summer Nights...

For Black Families in the south – Selma, South Chicago, Saint Louis, SW D.C. to name a few – the "oral tradition" of passing history from generation to generation happened on the front porch, sitting on the steps, in front of the drug store over checkerboards...or under the shade tree in the yard.

Summer nights were always the best when heat captured in the bricks chased us to the front porch and into the hot breeze that was much better than stagnant insides. We listened to stories better than the "Lone Ranger, the Green Hornet...": and other fictitious creations. Ours were true stories of family times. We lost ourselves in hours of laughter and popped corn – buttered, sweet and sticky with syrup. We licked our fingers and laughed loud enough to attract the rest of the family. We laughed 'til we cried.

Whatever the story, it was the job of the old ones remaining to recount the stories. They would expand on the "whoppers" or truths to sweeten the telling.

Today, so many of the black monarchs and matriarchs are gone and there's no one to pass on the legacy.

For this, I am deeply saddened and hope those who remain capture one or two of the stories to keep them from dying.

I'm told that this is a "deep concept – telling the history." But I wonder how deep can it be when it's just about a bunch of stories, about folks we know from stories told so often.
And after a while, it seems that we were carried through the cotton fields or ran ahead of the dogs – to freedom in the North. It's our story, and it's personal, and it should be in history books. But it's not.

I'll remember the stories when the popped corn is buttery and sweet again. I've got to teach my children to make popped corn with syrup. Maybe they'll remember my stories too.

We Sing the "Song of the Village"

In the 'melting pot' we call home, we must NOW reclaim "The Village Song" of our past when children were our legacy. Hold again in our hearts the spirit of the 'One', where each is just a small part of the whole. Reclaim the singular voice that chants of the almost forgotten histories – oft retold by matriarchs and warriors. Dust off our misplaced victories.

Raise the cry of the village in places where the huts have been replaced with asphalt and fiberglass. Here is where the village concept must be reborn – on streets, in alleys and concrete of Los Angeles, St. Louis and NYC.

"Never lost is the language of the forest and plains families and newly found is the language of brotherhood." These are the song lines that MUST be relearned and rewritten into the family Bibles. Ask 'Madea,' ask the reverends, ask the warriors, ask our fathers, in whose hearts our stories still survive. Sing again, the song of OUR village

Raise the cry of the village in places where the huts have been replaced with asphalt and fiberglass. Here is where the village

concept must be reborn – on streets, in alleys and concrete of Los Angeles, St. Louis and NYC.

The charismatic people must be revived – reborn in the next generation lest the song of the village die. Our family draws the strength of future hopes and dreams from past remembrances and promises – when "all my children" was more than a TV theme and 'we' was the concept that elevated our stature and bound us one to another

Raise the cry of the village in places where the huts have been replaced with asphalt and fiberglass. Here

Continued...

is where the village concept must be reborn – on streets, in alleys and concrete of Los Angeles, St. Louis and NYC.

In our future, when our legacy and our children cry out, "Where is my family?" We will reply that 'your family is here'…the global people that give color to the rainbow. We ARE the warrior people…the charismatic people…revived and reborn in a generation that now sings the song of the NEW Village. Here, the individual's success is OUR treasure. When our children cry out, "Who is my family?" We will shout, "We are ONE!"

Raise the cry of the village in places where the huts have been replaced with asphalt and fiberglass. Here is where the village concept must be reborn – on streets, in alleys and concrete of Los Angeles, St. Louis and NYC.

The 'Song of the Village' is OUR anthem. People of color; take you all the hands of a neighbor to reform our circle of life. The child in our midst is the focal point and may draw freely of our strength to complete the whole.

Raise the cry of the village in places where the huts have been replaced but the village concept is reborn – in our family united in cities from Los Angeles, to St. Louis and NYC.

Declaration of Independence...

Who am I to say..., it's all about me!

The world seeks out opportunities to put tape measures, and yard sticks, and calipers on judgment, thoughts and actions of every microbe. But I am above and below the radar and ignore all attempts to be measured or managed. I reject the boundaries and fences that attempt to contain the spirit of wildness and passion that lurks within. I push back and push down doors and reject rules that tell me who to be in my private times and publicly. But they are all private times in my mind. There is a statute of limitations on occupancy – only me in my mind – and that's my standard.

Only the experts know where to be or how to stand for something, or nothing, or everything they think important. I think not! I determine the stature of the man I am. I stand tall when others sit quietly and sit in silence when the world screams for attention. I know the limits of my skin and reject any attempts to stretch my
confinement to hold more than just me. I remain the only inhabitant of my skin and

the sole proprietor of the reflection in the mirror...down to the marrow – I continue to be the owner. Not you, but me.

The measure of this person is against standards that I erect on door frames and along mountain trails, and on sequoias that were here before the rules of modern society.

I am determined to spend a lifetime in my own head and about the same amount of time in my own birthday suit. I will be the body mechanic for me, and no one else will invade this space. Like everyone else, I will be running out of time and no time to live someone else's life or lie.

Continued...

So, who am I to say that you can't make decisions about my heart, my head or my feelings? Quite simply, "IT'S ALL ABOUT ME!"

Who I am, is a decision made by me that's not subject to discussion or your approval.
Get used to it!

Tomorrow...

Tomorrow there will be no slums because building materials will be in short supply and accelerated urban renewal will be repatriating the homeless to third world countries, or the outskirts of town.

Tomorrow there will be no poverty because of funding shortages and currency revaluation making money a moot (decimal) point moving with haste to the right as a fickle value for equality.

Tomorrow there will be no night clubbing by police in ghetto situations (PIGS), because "to protect and serve" will only apply to 'Dunkin Donuts' in need of new grease.

Tomorrow there will be no civil rights bills from Capitol Hill because of a sewer stoppage caused by recycling continuing resolutions to fund the bill of 64 again and again and again...

Tomorrow Justice will not be in because she will be on the corner watching tricksters turning their backs as usual, so that more shootings and jail time for a minority perspective will be a rebuttal to "his stories about just us in a Birmingham jail."

Tomorrow there may be no tomorrow for some, because of a power shortage... and poor planning, or a lack of desire to stay, when hope is out of town.

And Tomorrow there will be no shutting me down till "the story of right is retold...", and "Days of Our Lives" in syndication is rebroadcast with a new plot about 2016 when someone who really cares is elected and pigs fly. And tomorrow starts looking like a rerun of today in syndication.

TODAY, there will be no slums, because paper boxes and tents are mobile, and homeless is more than a concept.

See Me…!

My soul cries as you stare straight ahead in daily passage.
In your ignor(e)ance, do you think I am a speed bump to your success.
I am no ghost, although I was once the "Invisible Man."
Back in 'Nam – in the sixties, I was painted in green and (agent) orange.
"Endless night" hunting in narrow caves – covered in my brother's blood and
    foreign mud.

When I came home, I was different – broken in ways that frightened you.
People had difficulty seeing me – through the scars, the poverty and the pain
that hides me – still camouflaged, I sleep in city-caves that smell of refuse.
See me! Hear me!

My soul cries out, in days past, I was a son – your brother – a father and a hero.
I'm no commercial for Windex! Can't you see me!
I carry my valuables in a bag. This is not all I am.
I'm not a placeholder for pitiful. I used to be like you.
Though you look right through me, I used to act like you and block rays of light.
I was a man of substance.
Don't think my outstretched hand is there to pat you on the back for your lack of
    humanity.
It's not a branch or tree.
See me! Hear me!

My soul cries out that
Skid Row and the Bowery weren't always my vacation destinations.
In years past, I put on 3 pieces to suit the world that called me Mister.
My passage wasn't always in the back of paddy wagons.
Cops and ambulances weren't always making trash runs to drop off me and my
    friends.
Now they call taxis to take me to places invisible to you – out of sight.
Don't think that avoiding my eyes will make me disappear. I'm here to stay until
    change arrives!

Your shame should be about forgetting that I almost died for you,
    while your father planted seeds on a decade-long vacation in
    Canada.
See me! Hear me!

Continued…

My soul cries out
for help, but nobody knows where.
No MapQuest to go to the places I've been or even to find me now.
A distant leper island isn't so far-fetched to ease your guilt.
"Street people genocide" sounds like another case of "not my job" for 911 calls from an ER.
A chorus screams across the wire in hopes that someone will care enough to answer the plea.
Our war is not abroad, but at home in the streets.
My soul cries out that "I am not refuse or no use!"

SEE ME! HEAR ME!

Reflection on "See me...!"

In 1968, I traveled through Washington, D.C. while serving in the military. Until then, I was unaware that so many people could call the doorways of empty storefronts "home." I had no idea that a cardboard box could be such a valued shelter from the merciless winter cold. I was clueless that this pandemic existed everywhere in the world.

As the manifestations of the '60s and Vietnam brought me to new consciousness, I realized that this was one of many social constructs guaranteed NOT to discriminate by color. I was equally sure, that this was not just another losing concept from "The Hill," nor was it limited JUST to the "Chocolate City."

I was yet to realize how much bigger, more enduring and frightening than even the war, this problem would become. I was saddened, but as an 18-year-old I was very preoccupied with my chances of travel to Vietnam.

Almost 50 years later, I am still disheartened when I see people without hope, ignored like litter on the street. Each has become the new "Invisible Man" that Ralph Ellison would be writing about today.
This time the discrimination, bigotry, elitism, sense of entitlement, callousness and inhumanity IS identifiable in nanosecond soundbites as a "global poverty pandemic," and not limited to people of color in America.

Here in America, it transcends racial lines and partners with schizophrenia, depression, and PTSD – the new "Battle Fatigue." Ralph would probably suggest that NOT looking directly into their eyes, or NOT walking within 50 feet of them, will NOT make them disappear.

He would probably suggest that we "join forces and get a clue to figure out a new strategy!" He would not care about your sensitivity to my lack of sensibility when I see people who cross the street hoping that "they" will be relocated out of the park and out of sight.

It seems that some people of means who can get away won't be worrying about this problem until the chickens come home to roost and pigs learn to fly. That being said, I'd suggest that NOW is the time to fix the problem since there have been recent reports of chicken nests in upper-crust trees, and sightings in November 2016 of flying pigs near Capitol Hill.

When reality arrives in that neighborhood, on the heels of protesters, a "Time Machine" may be in the making. I am just saying, "Get to your nearest church, synagogue, temple or congregation. "

Hopefully, we will all arrive on the day the "LOVE, PEACE and JOY MESSAGE" is being taught. If that is a prayer and "Do you get it?" the final part of a sermon, then this invisible man says, "GOD HELP US!

AMEN!?"

WOMAN'S Lib

Liberate me...! Humph...!
Offer me something more tangible.
Give me something I have not.

I am a Black Goddess.
It was I that blew the first breath of life into Blackness.
It was I that you first feared, for you knew me not.
No chains could hold me, nor bonds enslave me.
I remain forever like the rustle of leaves, untamed, unrestrained
and free!
Liberate ME!?

Humph...! Give me something that I have not.
I am LIBERATION in the bravest sense; in its broadest meaning.

It was I that strode forward in battle to protect
the first and not the last BLACK seeds of Genius!
These were my Black Princes, whom you stole and tried to make
your own.
GIVE ME SOMETHING THAT IS YOURS TO GIVE!!!
Offer to me something that I did not myself give origin to...
Liberate ME!? Humph!

It was I that followed my sons – my PRINCES to your shores, and
gave them songs to place upon their lips, salves to cover their
welts, and defiance to fill their hearts.

It was I that bared my breast to their image in our first,
But not to be our last borne.
It was I that warmed their beds in winters from which there was no
shelter.

IT WAS I that heated the North Wind and blew a breath of strength into
their souls.

You dare to offer to me, what I myself am. HUMPFF!!
Give me something that I am NOT!!!

Continued...

It was I that steeled the mind of my Black Prince daily to the task of FREEDOM.
It was I that called him home, to stand valiant and strong at my side.

It is I who stands ever ready to meet his needs; that cries at his disappointments; that triumphs in his conquests, and who bemoans his injury.

You offer to me what you cannot give.
Give to me what I cannot.

I alone have all that you crave.
I have already been liberated.
I, the sister, the mother, the QUEEN, am LIBERATED!
Give me?
Humph…! It is what I give to myself.

Escape from Cape Coast Castle…

For some reason, memories of such dark places endure, even when witnesses are long buried. The smells – awful and rank, have been captured between threads of Kente cloth. Stitched together, they pass for histories – stories retold and repeated to generations of my people. They were, and are, the legacies of my kidnapped Ashanti cousins and reminders of the past.

Cape Coast Castle was our last view of home - long gone. My ancestors wailed from deep dark places. Surely, they mourned when even a place such as this passed from view and finally recollection. After all, it was home for a time, no matter how bad - our captors were sometimes our family.

The screams of my ancestors are captured *inside* museum pictures and imprisoned there for posterity. Their flesh drew back at the touch of whips, into bloody welts, as if retreating from a legacy of pain. Even now as I gaze upon these images, my spirit recoils from a memory not mine. This is my inheritance. This pile of rocks – the Castle, still stands as a reminder of enslaved tribes, shattered families and stolen kingdoms.

Cape Coast Castle was the last view of our home – long gone. My family still laments the losses. Surely, they mourned when even a place such as this passed out of recollection and out of hope. After all, it was home for a time, no matter how bad - our jailers were sometimes our family.

Although I do not remember it directly, I know that I must have come from proud people. My black skin is proof of my entitlement, just as this pile of rocks is an edifice to my plundered legacy. Family roots vanished as my people passed through "The Door of No Return." Future generations disappeared THEN, and NOW we follow a centuries-old trail back home to the Cape.

Cape Coast Castle is my first view of home – long gone and newly found. I sob now in a place where my ancestors once screamed. Surely, they would mourn the memories when a place such as this comes into view and into recollection. But the place these rocks now stand - no matter how bad, was once our home…long before it was our prison.

Birthrights... My Reflection is My History

Forgetting doesn't undo history and lying about the truth doesn't make it a new truth. Our story is alive and refuses to be silenced. Our chapter titles talk eternally of "Freedom", "Justice" and "Warriors with Honor."

The stories are both fact and fiction.
They remain long after yellowed pages are only dusty remains on hallway shelves. The history of entire nations refuses to die or be lied about as long as one matriarch lives, and retells the story at bedtime, or by candlelight.
The story is the history.

The history lives on with a direct link to the past ... in my flesh, in my reflection. I wonder what part of storytelling genetic and what part is undocumented cultural history.
IT refuses to die – perhaps a future vengeance on those who would bury the truth without a headstone.

The words of this story might as well be tattooed into my skin or woven into my naps – I know them by heart. I know, too, that my ancestors were no willing emigrants, and that is part of the story. But then I look into the mirror to see a "High Yella Brutha" with green eyes. Maybe they were emigrants and part of the untold history that lives in this reflection.

I wonder that I've NEVER seen a white face in the generations of blackness captured in scrapbooks on the coffee table. Perhaps they are in the crack of the pages, or my image belies it.

I can only imagine that some pretty sister didn't struggle, or moan, or raise an alarm as she became an unwilling vessel. This must have been the story and is the history. The reflection..., remember?

The history lives on with a direct link to the past ... in my flesh, in my reflection. She was allowed to live, and her slave husband was allowed to abandon his manhood.

Continued...

by Ronald Montgomery

The public emasculation of African Princes buried the sickle deep in black manhood for ten generations. Even today I feel the anger of the cold steel in private parts that follow me, and I wince in pain.

In this story, the seed grew, and repeated pain became the norm. The pain was her violation, and my pale complexion was a reminder that she was allowed to live and so was I.
I've been accepted and rejected but imprinted with the stigma - the history that nobody mentions in polite society, or at home in the family. This story is the history.

The history lives on with a direct link to the past … in my flesh, in my reflection. Forgetting is no cure…, only a salve. Lying to myself about the truth doesn't make it a lie.

My story is alive and refuses to be silenced.
I am a reminder of her sin? My history is her pain.

She was quiet and did not speak…saving me from a death that I did not merit.
She bore me in silence and held back her screams.
She was and so I am.
Nothing can change that, now. The story is the history. Her strength and pain is my legacy.

The history lives on with a direct link to the past …,
in my flesh, in my reflection.
My history and every chapter speaks of "Birthrights",
"Strong Mothers" and "Sisters with Honor."
She is what my woman will be – a queen set free
from the pain of unwanted history.

REFLECTION on "Birthrights..."

Kurotwamansa to nsuo mu a, ne ho na efo; ne ho nsensanee no de ewo ho daa. The translation is, "The leopard only gets wet when it falls into water; the water does not wash off its spots." The spots that make a leopard a leopard are the genetic history that is inescapable. My pale complexion and naps are my spots. I am who I am. Just as my leopard brother is a large cat.

This story is more complex than a first reading might suggest. It is more complex than the story telling in schoolbooks. The real history talks about the abuse of mothers, sisters and wives before, during and after the "door of no return."

The abuse was known. The sin was not hers. The stain was brought to light in the high-yellow pigmentation of her babies. Our past "Madea's" were truly warrior queens. Their strength is documented by the fact that so many raised and loved sons and daughters who remind them of their pain.

The true sin is that they were reminded daily that we – the children – were and are the instruments that inflict pain with reflections that we cannot change.

Today, these courageous women have no sin when they raise up a broken vessel (a child spared from abortion) within the sanctuary and dedicate the work He will do in him. This is my birthright. It is our birthright.

I speak now for the many with no voices then or now. We are no sin. Our history still lives on in our skin.

Dark Addiction

I was angry about giving up the things, the people I loved at a cost
A retrospective view of me was part of an unhappy fringe
Standing on the sidelines – looking at life as part of an alien place
A view of life's goings-on that I desired but could never have
A precious view that I could never embrace – no place for me
My third person, "He" was a light skinned brother
Blowing his wig back with a seven percent solution
Trying not to get his "cracked open behind" capped before getting high
Jus' sayin' that he'd rather be the can opener, than inside a can of whup
Or catching a case of something that lives in clinics or midnight jail cells
Or feeling cold hands clutching at his soul in some damp gutter
He knew many others and was known by all on the street
His sidekick was a black shadow and closer than skin
They hooped with me and my boys and was "Dude"
To those that didn't call him "Death…"
He was a vampire that lusted after a crack – the back of my elbow
And I gave in "satisfied" and gave him a home again and again
We wandered aimlessly and slept in a stupor together
Eating in binges and lamenting my movable crib – a dark gangway
There was no fear of what I embraced as the street taught me the game
On the outside "Gangsta" and inside banging, and popping too high
Trying to hustle myself into giving up the dreaded emptiness
And hiding a fear that my friend could never see
Since fear made him hungry and he smelled it oft in me

Still Smoking

When you came into my life you had that look about you.
You could have been black powder, or petroleum vapors.
The results would have been the same – explosive.

You were looking for an open flame to ignite you into final purpose,
and you were happy working diligently in my kitchen.
There you generated your own kind of oven, burner, and broiler heat.

You posted signs that were too near for me to read.
They warned of what I now know.
"Getting too close can result in deep and lasting burns."

And the last sign I remember seeing was
"I may not be young and hot, but I'm still Smokin'…"

KABOOM!!!

"Wild Butterflies"

Dreams soar to the skies on silken wings of longings, desires and windswept kisses.
In hurried meetings, and secret escapes we seek a haven, a heaven – a place to put our hearts to rest from endless flights of fancy.

Our captive hearts are embraced by enchanted webs spun by wispy kisses.
We build dreams of finding a home for our reality shaped by love's journeys and a stopping place for our hearts.

Our souls always touching, we are free.
We are sometimes closer than others, but always in a state of belonging and longing for each other.
When we reach each other and touch, we fly higher and cavort.

The flight of wild butterflies are we…

by Ronald Montgomery

CoCo's Kingdom

Cheetahs run to be at your side with wolves, trumpeting elephants, and fuzzy bears.
They inhabit the wild kingdom – the bedroom that you rule – and your bed, a plateau surrounded by unexplored territories. Your closet, an untamed jungle, provides refuge for undiscovered treasures and jewels – all buried from view and possible recollection.

Wild sounds drift on occasion from the crack of the almost closed door of your kingdom. They are joined by your voice singing siren songs and lilting melodies that only your minions and explorers may hear – all adding to nature calls and musical sounds of the jungle.

And I, the daring hunter – the manager and sometimes naturalist of the reserve, and most often your father, have tried taming and making you a stuffed bear or lioness that sits calmly, quietly, and civilized on **MY** shelf, only to find you untamable and wild...

I smile with resignation, knowing that once I had a wild kingdom, too.

Cheerleaders *in Aprons*

Can you imagine cheerleaders in aprons...? We all have them.
Most often they're the woman who sacrificed her lap... to OUR heads...
She's the one who rubbed OUR backs to ease the pain of OUR splinters and bloodied knees.
She's Mom, mother, MADEA.

They are so complex.
At times, they are the voice of rough and stern when raising children alone, and THEN they are the shelter that we run to... when ONLY HER TWO ARMS are enough to encircle and protect us, and to fix a problem no one else can see.

They are cinnamon, ginger, homemade vanilla ice cream, and the condensed sweet milk she uses for hot chocolate.
Ummmmmmmm. So good.

Sometimes it seems we are too young to really understand the significance of her love. And at other times, it seems we are too preoccupied with our own lives and growing up to even care. But, loving us as ONLY a "REAL" mother loves... she hopes that a series of "TENDER moments" will stick in our memories... and THESE will be the signposts, and markers in our lives, WHEN WE KNOW that we were loved by you... These memories will be OUR respite when we too pray for an angel, for wisdom, for love and for renewal.

I still remember the words of my mother.
These are HER words..., and the words I heard as she rocked my children on her sometimes-swollen knees.

She'd say, "I love you more with EACH breath and longer than THIS life. I prayed for your father and now I pray for you." Mama, today I blame you – I BLESS you for great the joy I feel and the gratitude I know... when I thank God for making me your child.

You told me that it was no accident...
That God made me for you... You said...

Maybe some song's lyrics could say it better than I...
"But, You ain't no accident, God made you for me."

When "lonely" filled my heart and I needed someone to hold, I prayed for an angel and then you came.

When "hope" was in short supply and doctors uncertain..., I prayed for a miracle and then you came.

When "wisdom" was out of reach and "smart" was its substitute, I prayed for an answer and then you came.

When "Faith" was a name and Abraham my best reference, I prayed for a mustard seed and then you came.

Continued...

When "Love" was a feeling and physical was all I knew, I prayed for "REAL" and then you came.

When "Life" made me cry and all my accounts were empty, I prayed for "Renewal" and then you came.

Patti sang a love song that really hit the mark ...
She said "When you've been blessed pass it on..."

Momma, I will give to my children the love you gave....
I am blessed, knowing that God made you just for me...

One day, I will tell MY grandchildren

"Once upon a time..., in Saint Louis, your grandmother
said these words to me, so that I COULD say them to you... "

"I love you more with EACH breath and longer than THIS life."

Tell your children, what I have told you and THEY can PASS IT ON!

PASS IT ON!!!

Home Again

There's no going home again.
There are just memories of what might have been
and a "One Way" street map – all moving away from
yesterday in the direction of now.

There's no going home again.
Feasts of yesterday are recipes of unique.
The ingredients are best guesses and wishes – all
smudges with no way to recreate the tastes that are
now only remembered smells of roasting feasts
dissipating in the wind.

There's no going home again.
Life departs and is never recovered.
There are only memories of the essence to taunt us
in forgetful days.

There's no going home again.
Just whirlwinds in the dust and footprints in the sand
eroded by surf and wind – only memories of where
our hearts have been.

There's no going home again.

Psalm of the Heart-Fortress...

Guard your Heart as a fortress. It is a seat for the **King**.
Though the war is won, battles rage on 'til all is done.
This song is witness to one of recent thousands that continue on and on.

Happy came along and hailed to the gatekeeper, "Lower the *bridge* for entry!"
But it had a Trojan relationship with *Deceit* and had no good intentions for the *Heart-Fortress*.

Seasoned, the soldiers on the wall were trained up to skepticism.
They held fast and secured the entry and fortified the walls with *Discernment*.
"Beware!" they shouted and paid no attention to the *World's Reality*.
The Soldiers commanded all, "Guard your *Heart-Fortress*! It can be deceived!
We wait for *Eternal*, accompanied by Joy and Peace. They will come hand-in-hand!
They come shortly. Endure!"

Pretty-Sounds and *Words* assaulted the gates and lullabied *All* within earshot.
"Let me in" it crooned. "I have come with *Pleasure* and *Happiness* to excite you, in your times here.
There is no risk. Lower your guard and I will fill you!"

Seasoned warriors prepared for battle by filling their ears with waxed *Wise-Words* for this occasion.
They sang songs and praised the *Teacher-King* for preparation in this day and sealed the gates.

The Strong-Warrior shouted to *All*, "Guard your *Heart-Fortress*! It can be deceived!
Heart-Ears wait for True-*Word*, accompanied by Joy and Peace. They will come hand-in-hand!
They come shortly. Endure!"

Finally, *Lust* attempted to catapult the walls for entry and to entice the lonely within.
"Hold me," it moaned. "See me. I am here for you. Feel my caress and remember me with your eyes.

Continued...

Do not be afraid, we are no strangers. I am familiar. My feelings cannot hurt you..."

Armored for the battle that must surely come, the *"Faithful"* comforted one another.
They fortified the walls where breaches and cracks appeared and smote her relentlessly into retreat.

They chanted to each other, "Guard your *Heart-Fortress*! It can be deceived!
Heart-Eyes await True-Love, accompanied by Joy and Peace. They will come hand-in-hand!
They come shortly. Endure!"

The battles raged on for what seemed *Forever-Minutes* to *Victory* – 'til all was won.
"We are Seasoned Warriors," they shouted. "We have prepared for battle. Hear the trumpets of the Warrior-King. He returns for the faithful.
Guard your Heart as a fortress and a seat for the KING!"

They sang songs and praised the returning *King* for his preparation for this day.

The Strong-Warriors shouted, "The throne within our *Heart-Fortress* is ready!

Make way! Make way! Make way! HE comes!!!"

Only from here...

The journey home begins here.

You asked me how to find the way to that place of perfect peace and tranquility. You are seeking the place where opportunity and purpose will intersect to show your part in His plan. You wonder which direction is right.

I can only tell you what He's shown me. Each path is unique. No one stands in for me, just with me. On my path, I sometimes hold hands and embrace others to keep from falling when left to my own devices. Sometimes, I find myself in the company of angels, but eventually they too depart.

In the end, you and I can only get to that place that we seek from here. And the journey does not begin tomorrow, but yesterday, and the days before when we first began to recognize a path beneath our feet. We traveled even when we had no idea where the path would lead.

You ask, "How does it feel to know the plans for your life?"
I tell you, there are so many things I have yet to know about my place, the plan and my life. The certainty of tomorrow is a guess and things hoped for, for sure. So surely, I don't know about tomorrow, and only He and I know the "now" of my plan. Today my certainty is that the rest of my journey begins here and in this moment that I call "now."

What I am certain of, is that I cannot get to the ordained appointment from anywhere but here. Yesterday's path is gone and directly ahead is the visible path for me.

You ask, "How long is the path? How far will I have to go to reach the goal?" I tell you that yesterday I sat in sand stretching as far as the eye can see. I looked for an oasis, and wondered how many steps it would take, not knowing the path or direction. But today, I look to the distance with a single palm tree in view.

As I approach, more is revealed with each step that draws me nearer. The way is a narrow path that gets me to the goal, but only from here. I find that following the path requires endurance, as I finally reach the oasis.

Continued...

You ask me, as I sit at the water's edge, if I have reached my goal. I tell you truly, although the water is sweet and cool, and I am quickened, this is only a resting spot en route to "my appointment."

In a play, the details are revealed to the audience as the plot unfolds. There is no way to speed the delivery to get to the conclusion. The path is revealed only through the journey.

You ask me, when will you have the success that I have? Today I laugh at this. Like you, I have asked Him the question, "Why am I such a failure?" His reply to an adopted son was, "How can you be a failure if you are part of My Plan?" This is His answer to me.

I tell you that I do not know the answers to your question, but I do know that He speaks to his children.
Following the narrow path is a journey of faith. If

this sounds unfamiliar to you, then you will find yourself resting until you are ready to continue without knowing your next step.

He says that He will guide the steps of the righteous. The steps are ordered. I tell you, look to the future from here. The desert will give way to the oasis. The mountains will give way to the plains. The seas will give up dry land. On the journey, even your uncertainty will give way to an abiding peace if you have faith.

In rough times, do not despair. He will send a host of angels to walk with you – to protect you on the way "to your

appointed place." If you only know one more thing, know that you and I can only get to our divine appointments from here. But your time and place are not mine.

Truly, I tell you... You will not be late, and He will be on time. SELAH!

by Ronald Montgomery

Reprise

Life In just a minute...

A lifetime has evaporated into no time at all.
Where have all my *"nows"* gone?
For hours, I relive the lingering first touches of passion while in the moment.
I remember as if just yesterday and savor hundreds of life's sweetest entrées.
In that yesterday, I went from playing with dolls to playing with an angel that bore my joys and pains.
I beheld a child that bore my name and looked through hazel eyes at a miniature copy of me.
I've lived my life in just a minute. And in that minute, I found my reasons for being here.

A lifetime has dissolved into no time at all.
Where have all my *"todays"* hidden?
The time won't be stretched or compressed, even though it seems like only a minute ago that I tugged at my father's coat.
It was only a blink later when I stole a first kiss on your front porch.
And wasn't it just yesterday, 40 years and one tear later we kissed our last kiss – I held on to delay your escape.
I've lived my life in just a minute when I found my reasons for being here.

A lifetime has changed into no time at all.
What's become of my *"yesterdays?"*
For what seems an eternal now, I hold onto the dance when I first felt you breathing against me – as you pressed against my thigh and I hid my excitement. It was that yesterday when I was anchored in the moment and dug-in with my heels to slow the pace.

I've lived my life in just a minute when I found my reasons for being here. A lifetime has changed into no time at all.
Where are my *"tomorrows?"* The time won't be slowed to make exquisite and tasty languish on my tongue.
The smell of beauty set free by wild flowers, won't linger once in flight with the wind, or in league with seasons past.

Continued...

Could it have been just yesterday, when I spied a monarch perched atop the tallest blade of grass, as it pushed winds with massive wings and rested from a long flight?

I've lived my life in just a minute and discovered that a lifetime is no time at all.
Where has all the time gone?
And now it's time to go.

Chapter 2

"Unfortunately, understanding life with the result of wisdom, doesn't always begin at LESSON ONE…, or chapter one, for that matter.

I'm told often, by those older than me, that wisdom comes later in life to those who seek it and ONLY in the sequence of life's days.

So, as I work on understanding life, I continue to look for wisdom under grains of sand in deserts and on beaches – behind blades of grass in meadows and fields.

And while I wait for "later in life" to arrive with a portion of "Wisdom," I will begin writing Lesson One, Chapter Two.

Nun's Prayer (Love Lost)

"A nun seeking release from her vows."

I pray a nun's prayer dear God.
I have read Luke, emulated Job, and read from Genesis to Revelation.
Much do I marvel at the poetry of Your voice set to man's hand.
But, read as I do and memorize as I have Your precepts, no comfort do I find
- no love.
Give me strength.

Your arms do not hold me, and Your voice does not soothe me.
Your face leaves no burning image in my mind but love You I do.
Give me strength.

Oh Lord I have closed my mind to "self" thoughts that warm me,
with countless "Hail Marys, Our Fathers, and Kyries", but this was not
enough. I cringe at the awesome might of Your deeds, that no ruler could
measure - that surely no man could equal.
Give me strength.

But awe is not enough and might need I not.
Nothing as small as a mustard seed, nor riches of gold and jewels, but rather
the peace of mind, and the riches of affection...
Give me strength.

I have prayed for your strength to obscure my weakness of "One".
My Lord even You were lonely - so You created a world; of woman You
begot a son and left us the Holy Spirit as a comforter. I thank You.
But no comfort do I find.
Give me strength.

To a son You keep loving at Your side
You made me Your bride...
But He has loved me from afar, Lord.
He loves me not, Father - not as a woman.
And I am lonely... No litany fills the emptiness.
My Lord, my Liege, give me leave.

JUNKMAN

As I peered through the screen on an autumn morning, I heard his wheels rattling on the cobblestones - making a distinctive sound, as he moved a huge cart on the strength of his back, legs, and cracked fingers in a life of no make believe.

His corners began in the middle of the blocks, and his "Time Square" of intersecting alleys was desolate, and saw no fireworks save the sparks of steel rims brushing against bricks and rocks.

His personage was that of a prophet out of date, and his carriage that of a fallen angel.

His face was carved from rock with little flesh to soften the breaks and cracks of his wrinkled skin and was shielded by a salvaged brim that gave little sight. His back bent to the load and leaned to the wind, as he passed down the alley behind my house.

His face was a mystery to the world that passed unnoticed by a proper world and forgotten now in what seems a fable. His passage was unnoted except by the absence of rags, bottles, and ill-fated waste — his booty piled high — to which he was a savior, disappeared from view as he pulled away.

His clothes were threadbare shambles that held together his frame and gave him form that covered his nakedness, and rebuked the elements for their lack of mercy, and mankind for progress since his day was past. He bent to the load and leaned to the wind.

His shoes were a wonder. Though torn and worn, they magically suspended his feet above glass and nails, protecting his steps.
They gripped the cracks and propelled him forward from stop to stop of new treasures piled ever higher on the heap.
They left no prints or impressions to be seen or remembered by...

His was an exercise in identity...
A gnarled willow he bent even lower in search of some yet unknown new treasure. And finding none he leaned again into the wind and bent to a load which he pulled, to a distinct rattle of cobblestone and steel, slowly out of view and out of time.

by Ronald Montgomery

"a letter to god"

hello god,
my name is johnnie. i am 12 years ole and i live in kabreenie green. im only telling you where i live so youll know exactly where to look to find me, because chicago is a big city, with a lot of people. im on the third floor of the tenemant house on 33rd street. my room faces out on the fire escape toward the street. so you wont
get me mixed up with my two younga bruthas. im oldes and the larges to. i really dont know if you are who mom says you are and i really dont know if you really can do the things she says you can, but ive decided to write you a letta and get the facts. tell me something bout yourself.

its kinda hard sometimes to believe all of the things people tell you all the time, cause it seems that most of the time, they talk off the top of their heads. and i wonda sometime if they really believe it themselves.

i see mom cryin sometime, real quiet like in the
kitchen or maybe while shes doin housework. she don't make a sound and if i didnt know betta id think that she just got done washin her face and forgot to dry it. but i know cause im hip to whats goin on. i walk up and i put my arm around her sholda, and thats not so hard
to do, cause i'm almost as tall as her now,
and i ask her what's wrong. she usually

dont say much cep god loves us. i really dont
know what thats means. shes been sayin it for
years but it dont seem to help nothin, she just keeps on sayin and keeps on cryin. and things just keep on gettin rufa.

what color are you? do you look and act the way mr. jones does. in case your wonderin who mr. jones is, hes the supa. he pounds on the door on the fust of the munth. hes been poundin on the door for as long as i can memba. sometimes i could swear i hear the hinges comin out the doe. he pounds and he pounds.

Continued...

mr. jones talks loud and says nasty things to mom. he used to say the same nasty things to my daddy, until one day my old man pulled his piece out and promised to blow his m.f. brains out and then a little while layta the pigs came and took him away.

im not supposed to use words like that but i figue its alright since im writtin you. if youre like mr. jones, im usin words youll undastand. mr. jones is fat and white and looks real greasy. he lives down on the fust floor with his wife. they aint got children. mr. jones even hollas at his wife. i know these things cause the walls and floors are like tissue paypa. i know that one of these days im going to have to kill mr. jones because of the way he pounds on the door and talks to my mom. but thats goin to be afta i get enough money to get a gun. if youre like him i may have to kill you to.

i hope youre not. are you cold? i mean are you nice or are you cold?

i saw the man on the block again yestaday. hes
cold. hes very cold. you dont see nothin in his face his name is d. he dont talk to kids. he just talks to his boys. joe used to skin pop with the stuff he got from d but now hes mainlinin. joe died yestaday. d found out that he was holdin out part of the stash and gave him some bad stuff. d is cold. are you like that? if you are, i cant deal with you.

maybe youre not like etha one of them. maybe
youre like the president. he suppposed to be a big shot. he knows a lot so i hear and he runs every bodys lives. but he dont know me and i dont know him. he passed some paypa last week that said that mom couldn't get no more money to buy food for us, so i guess maybe
ill have to bet out on the streets and get into some big money. im not sure what ill do, but ill do something big enough to take care of mom.

the president is cold to, in a way. hes like you so
mama says. hes far away and you neva see him. or at least i neva seen him and neetha has mom. hes like you i guess, only a picture on the wall in the paypa, or maybe a picture people carry around in their head. are you real? pictures dont make things real. people dont make things real just by talkin about them. people lie a lot.

Continued...

take al for instance. he told me he saw you in church last
week. he must have been lyin, cause i didnt hear nothin
about it and if you was
as big as they say you are, it would have been in the
newspaypa. — you see what i mean? so u see that's why im
writtin you...to get to the bottom of this thing...

who you are? please tell me who you are, so that i can
recognize you when i see you. if you really are. please write
me very soon so i can start lookin. thank you very much,

ronnie

p.s. i dont know how much stamps cost, and if i did i dont
have money, so youll have to pay it. ill
give it back to you sometime.

The WORD

    You take me for granted and act as if you can sling me, compress me, and
        pull me in every direction
to suit your selfish needs. In your meager understanding, you seem
        unaware of my beginning.
I waited patiently for you to crawl from the oceans and caves to discover
        me and not the other way around.
Fast forward a thousand lifetimes or more, and you would have seen me
        waiting, pondering, and
molding the expression of your stick drawings, of your art and finally
        erupting as building blocks for nations.
You heard me as high praises – an enticement to nations and exaltation to
        throngs, while
in private you whispered "Me" to satisfy mean cravings.
Never think that you will outlive my usefulness. I will remain LONG after
        you have departed
Your progeny will try to use me up and I will outlive them, too. I brought
        you forth from the firmament
into existence! I was your Genesis.
Now you use me as a hammer and a tool to sledge into cracks with blunt
        force trauma what should not be,

and then you forget that I am more nuanced than you understand and
    for meanings, you cannot imagine.
I am recessed in stone, raised in dots on paper and will be here when
    you have been forgotten and lay
moldering in the dust.
On the last day when "Well done, good and faithful servant" is uttered,
    I will come forth to do
His bidding – to reward the good and punish the wicked for the words,
    turned to deeds, that have lived in the
heart's abundance – that have escaped from pursed lips and tongues to
    "Light" or "Darkness."
If some brazen concept thinks itself more powerful than the "Word," let
    it step forward to discover that ONLY
the creation – Words on His breath – give form to ALL from void.

So sayeth He.

Forgiveness

The goal is changing me, never you.
Ahhhhh, there's the challenge of a lifetime.
It is a promise to forget but never the reality.
Come inside my heart and make yourself at home.
It is the only place where "forgiveness" is NOT on loan.

by Ronald Montgomery

In 1968, we the people (of color) were still living through and recollecting memories too recent to be called history. We watched and marched as people were dying (in church bombings) for the right to attend school, to sit at lunch counters, to ride buses and sit in any seat, and to not hang from branches in front of burning crosses because our skin color allowed us to blend into the night.

One Perfect Day

ONE PERFECT DAY
ONE PERFECT DAY
ONE PERFECT DAY
ONE PERFECT DAY

SHAKESPEARE

Had I the chance to claim as mine the
role of Shakespeare, in days gone by, I would
write, recite, and act out for the multitudes,
the finest of my creations...

I would stroll from
side to side on make-shift stages, and draw
forth from countless pages the feelings that would
    leave the audience
breathless, at your slight exertion, and would
render them bleeding, cursing, and half dead in
the aisles at the pain of your indignation.
They would only recover in time for my next act.

They would shudder at our fear, and escape
to the backs of their seats in your horror.
They would drown in the depths of our feelings,
and know no death sweeter. And at my words they
would climax on a kiss.

Multitudes would thrill to our embrace,
and feel no trace of fear that lurks at every turn.
They would pine at silent yearning that found
no voice... and sit without choice in the plot
we have etched with our lives.

My moments of despair would cause them countless
    hours of anguish.

Our happiness would create boundless satisfaction,
    contingent only upon my words, implanted in their
    minds and anchored in their hearts.

If only mine was the chance, to play the role...
of Shakespeare,...as me.

Diamond Studs...

Pierced ear-studs, searching for lobes...
The right and left remembrances of a tryst
Passing fancies, gone missing in a playful moment of passion...
Now rest on a bookshelf in search of naked ears
And nestled in repose – on fluffy clouds in a gift box...
Awaiting another special event...
Your return

Under Construction

While my mind is under construction, there will be a
station-break — a pause for the cause – an
intermission of sorts.

For the next twenty seconds, minutes, or decades
my mind will be out of tune.
There will be no reruns, just commercials,
No three-star matinees or soap operas.
No stars and stripes sign-offs.

My picture will be out of focus.
No new picture tube will make it better.
The test pattern will not be a rainbow peacock, but a
blank expression.

Do not talk, yell, or scream.
Do not disturb — until I get it all together.

Ommmmm...
Ommmmm...
Ommmmm...

Hello...

Reflection on "Under Construction"

In my youth, life was traveling at the speed of light. The memories in retrospect are blurred. It's almost as if my brain went into overload and finally woke from a deep slumber.

My sense is that I struggled to wake from a dream. When I woke, I was finally a sentient being. A metamorphosis had occurred – much like a butterfly emerging from the cocoon.

Arnett (J.J.), Hogan (D.P.) and Jensen (R.), et. al. have written scholarly articles about the transition to adulthood. Research is such wonderful stuff.

However, the research didn't arrive in my life prior to the personal realization that I had changed, absent input from anyone else. I felt fully aware for what seemed the first time in my life. By that time, I was well into my 40's with two children.

I felt, that I had squandered so much youth, time, relationships and opportunities as payment for wisdom. It wasn't as just a function of intellect, but also a spiritual awakening. I realized that we are all connected in deep energetic and spiritual ways, and that ultimately we share the same fate, regardless of class or color.

We will all reach the end of life and leave behind a legacy to be celebrated or mourned.

Bicentennial Student Rebellion

No Plato, no Socrates,
No Plutarch, no more.
Just "Siege," and Hughes, and Richard Wright;
a song for Billy Dee.
No pragmatism, no euphemism,
No more "O Say Can You See."
Just the "Invisible Man",
"The Man Who Cried I Am",
Oliver, Bird, and Coltrane:
The sounds that say I'm me.
No lecture halls or quad malls
No frat or sorority meetings.
Just city slums and ghetto walls...,
rats, minus health and heating.
No registration, no indoctrination.
No forms, formulas, or SATs.
Just kicking ass, and burning trash...
In the war on "POVERTY'.
No forty acres,
No plow, no mule.
Just tar and feathers,
Hanging ropes, and chains,
with no-justice, Just us, our guarantee.
No friendly faces, no education,
No deseg or equal races.
Just Malcolm, Martin and Angela
With an old message, re-written...,
"My mind will make me free."

Reflection on "Bicentennial Student Rebellion"

Living in the '60s and '70s, as a young person 'of color' was a challenge on many levels. These were my formative years.

In 1968, we the people (of color) were still living through and recollecting memories too recent to be called history. We watched and marched as people were dying (in church bombings) for the right to attend school, to sit at lunch counters, to ride buses and sit in any seat, and to not hang from branches in front of burning crosses because our skin color allowed us to blend into the night.

We the people (of color) were still living through and recollecting one-way trips to the places less than a day's ride from the DMZ (demilitarized zone in Vietnam). We watched as planes flew overhead dropping defoliants on the jungle twenty yards away and smelled the overspray as it wafted outward and finally reached us. This was an interesting smell, that "they" said wouldn't harm us, but would expose the enemy (...other people of color – "Gooks") for a "just conflict."

We the people (of color) lived in a time after the newest civil war, during the newest war on poverty and in the era of the *new intellectual* when we though the labels on our collective forehead were gone, and the doors of freedom and equality were unlocked.

These were the days when each day was followed by the next cliff-hanger – bringing us the days during and after Malcolm, Martin, JFK and Bobby left us. I discovered, to my naïve surprise, that the recently eradicated pejorative labels still left a visible impression, and that the doors without locks had cipher codes on the doorknobs not meant for me.

The deceptions were not just for me. The new and the old reality were the same, with a different name. The realization that the battles and the war for equality were far from over, was a wakeup call for me and other who thought "things are going to get better."

This realization gained strength and clarity over the next six years during which time I spent my days in dark places working for an agency with a three-letter acronym. I went to places with no names and sealed my lips and deadened my tongue..., for a minute. I was part of the machinery that created misinformation and called it fact. I was not pleased with me, or with lies that I knowingly co-authored.

Continued...

In 2016, I reread my own poetry and repeatedly ask the question, "What has really changed?"

I am also rereading "The Invisible Man," "The Spook Who Sat by the Door" and "The Man Who Cried I Am." When I have finished these, I will reread "The Fire Next Time."

Now I understand and recognize the mechanisms of deceit. The deceptions carry with them a rank stench that still lingers in the halls of Just-Us and in my nostrils.

So now, in retrospect when looking back at these decades of my life, I know beyond a doubt that there are messages and lessons here for us as a people and for me as a change agent. The doors that keep others out, become a prison for those inside. We are all "Colored" and "Exclusion" makes prisoners of us all.

Lesson Four

In this life, it seems I've been several individuals —
young and insincere, and old and austere.
And in each life, I've described myself as a messenger.
But, what was it... the message?
Was "it" an answer, or a question?
Before I leave this place, I'd like to know that it was
clear and made my trip here a success.
If you got it, please tell me, so that I can stop worrying.

Was the message for you or for me?

When...?

When did it stop . . .
the running to the door,
to grab at your coat,
All arms and legs we hung at your throat,
and tugged at your pants, and broke
out the smiles . . .
Where did they go . . .
the presents you bought
home from work;
red whistles, blue balls,
books and games.
Where did it end . . .
the hours end on end;
the times after dinner that we played in your
hair, combing and scratching all snug
in your chair.
Where did it stop..., the love?
When?

"NEVER... Just remember when I smiled."

Lesson Two

My children, my family and friends...
You are all my catalysts for new beginnings.

You may never know that I've written these lines for and because of you.

Likewise, I might never know the monumental efforts you've made for me when my back was turned.

Now, I am looking in the rearview mirror, and I see you and what you have done with me in mind.

Nothing stays hidden forever so turn the page and discover what I never told you.

A Passion for Living

For me, there will be no stopping, just stretching upward to the
 heights, my arms and heart can REACH
Not looking for relief, just release – like petroleum refined to vapors,
 in search of SPARKS
Like lightning spreading venous to clouds far and near, followed by
 thunderous applause RESOUNDING
An existential creativity hurling paint at moving canvases, walls and
 air for new EXPRESSIONS
Never accepting "satisfied and complete" as my mantra – there is no
 retreat from NEWNESS
Always planting seeds in fertile fields that yield forests, NOT solitary
 trees, for a bountiful HARVEST
Expressing irrepressible needs as unbridled forces to embrace and
 create works of LAUGHTER
Not standing still but leaning forward as the wind lifts me and
 teaches me to fly ever HIGHER
Every day searching for paradise lit by sunbeams - followed by
 nightlights on guided tours of WONDER
PASSION, an expression of amazement because my spirit sees
 tomorrow as the first day of FOREVER

Burning Embers…

An invitation to renewal…

For relighting the pilot in my life, that warms the
Mediterranean for a midnight swim…, I thank you.

For being a muse, that fans an ember promising
flames and heat to hold off the chill of the night…, I
thank you.

Step in — join me.
The water's just perfect and
the campfire is ready.

Move closer if you dare…

Alone

From my world within,
I am separate and apart.
With nothing to confuse me,
I'm doing quite well without.
Locked away in solitaire.
Locked within the confines of my mind.

Inspiration

Huh? Surprise!
A slap to the side of the head!
Not what I thought, but more than
any expectation and from some
unknown source – a place of
energy and light, where
Emerils, Rodins, Monets and
Hemingways concoct from whisks,
chisels, colors, and quills, new words,
works, and new worlds –
delivering to an unsuspecting me,
the "unimaginable" riding atop
a three-million-volt bolt of static AHA!
The lights are now ON!
BEHOLD! The void now waits to be
filled with another inspiration and
another creation!
I am ready!

Chula... (Pretty Baby)

PB — Chula de mi Vida...
This is a love letter waiting to be found by ONLY you.
If you're reading this and there's a smile on your face, then maybe I've succeeded in making your day a little brighter.
And knowing that your hands are holding this paper, my day will be sweeter. I will smile too. And whether I talk to you or not, I'll feel warm, holding you close in my heart.

This note to you will probably never inhabit the library of congress. But, I would be privileged beyond belief to have these pages placed in your shoebox of letters beneath your bed, or just remembered lovingly, on cold nights in front of the fire.

So, if you're reading this 50 or 60 years from now, know with assurance that someone cared for you enough to reread these words many times just to be sure "I love you" was spelled correctly.

And, if by chance you find this message while rereading the contents of your shoebox and are warmed by the embers that created these words, you can always call me collect on 555-1212.

I will be waiting for you to find this page, as I sit by the phone hoping it will ring for me, from you.

I love you.
Me

Reflection on "Pretty Baby"

For anyone who might not have been alive in the last century, dialing 555-1212 preceded by an area code was 'MA Bell's' network code for getting *long distance information.*

Long Distance? What's that?

"Not a local call. One that requires that you input an area code?"

MA Bell? Who is she? Local Call? What's that?

"Never Mind... Have I opened a can of worms? No, you can't buy them at the 'Save Way'. Oh never mind!
Forget it!"

Whatever...

Pretty Baby, if you are reading this please know that in paradise, I will not require a phone to hear from you. I will simply know that you tried to dial the number and I will be glad that you cared enough to call.

Remember the saying, "Here's a dime. Go call someone who cares...?"

I left a roll of new dimes in your jewelry box, so that you can call me. I do...

"Paradise Lost…".

Wispy clouds cover my mind's eyes…
But I remember, seeing you rise…, tugging you softly
  to stay…
Staring as you prepare naked beauty to leave our
  castle

Knowing recollections may fade…, I scribe
Challenging and pressing into submission, words that
  evade daily routines
Questions, "Were there ever really, our linked
  shadows on wet sand here…?"

In concert, colluding memory foam required to
  forget us both, resists butt fails
Fighting, it will prepare for the next set of royals
  arriving at noon, too soon
While once iced magnums with nectar remnants,
  recycle, amid rebellious clinks…, clanks

Almost abandoned Victoria holding secrets – at
  home now in my breast pocket
Not to be forgotten, rewards with whiffs, sweet
  perfume – keepsakes of love surrendered
A prelude to a dramatic bag drag – a hooptie awaits
  to frugal "Practical Times"

We've packed zero-dollar collectables, tagged and
  stored, "butt" invaluable
The price paid - the cost of hearts and noses opened
  wide, we depart with memories
Amid fond regrets for a too brief stay in paradise

An XX Autobiography

My Maleness has Mis-In-Formed Me
About A fish out of water, as I stand on the Edge
Hungry and with a Strong Appetite for Love…
I Read Returned Love Letters from This War

They are Memorized Out Loud Songs I've Never Sung
To be Worn Scratches in Vinyl for My Favorite Verse
Still Dis-Content with My Heart's Demands…
I Shout from the Jaws of the Beast pulling me out

These are Life's Illusions, Not Quite What They Seem
Like the Graffiti wrinkles on a Soft Headboard
Not Yet Having the Wisdom to Reform my heart…
I wonder, Have I been here before…, And Who are You?

Simple Pleasures

Ice cream and candy on a palette demanding more and more, in a life with no end to delight
Beautiful colors and art spread across the sky with no hand in sight
Long drives down a winding 101 – an ocean view of waves and Hearst, with just the right amount of sunlight
Chocolate melted on fingertips and thrust without regret to a waiting palette – warm and wet
Cold wine aloft on crystal thin stems to reflect light through perfect shades of amber and red
Arm-full embraces of warmth and caring to remember forever and ever
Expanding fullness in my soul to hold full measures of friendship and unconditional love
Senses all sent from above for boundless soulful delights for life-giving living

Story of a Free Bear

In my early days, I left my Father's house to become a "Free Bear..."

I thought that His rules only bound me and separated me from those who had fun in their lives.

I wanted to have fun and be happy, too.
I played in the streets, not caring about cars and trucks that whizzed by me.
Their nearness in inches only added to the excitement of doing dangerous things.

In those risky times, I misplaced my spirit and parts of my heart.
I thought I would wander those streets forever.
I went from boulevards to highways, knowing that the danger was major and so were the thrills.

I counted on skillful dodging to move me in the nick of time – believing I would easily jump from peril to safety.
My new way of looking at things, made any transgressions small.
I thought that breaking the law was mended by doing good deeds, on occasion.

I continued to play in unsafe ways because I believed I would never die. And I thought in the last moment I could leap to the safety of my Father's arms...

He beckoned me to sanctuary from the sidewalk.
But, I thought I wanted to wander those streets forever.
My appearance belies the fact that fifty-plus years ago, I left His house.
I've managed and manipulated, dodged and darted, and almost tarried too long.

And now I find the elements and time, have taken their toll.
I've weathered storms and cold, and blistering heat to be among those like me.
Living this life, I've watched seasons and my youth come and go.

Continued...

Some who weren't as quick have died and some have been crippled.
Some have simply gone away…, but I know not where.
In my haste, I moved to a street where I was alone in traffic – heavier than any I'd known.

It seemed I would wander those streets forever.
But even with all the bustle, I've found time to think of what might have been…
In my Father's house, what would my fate have been, had I never wandered these streets?

The streets no longer beckon to me and fun is no fun at all.
My head spins from all the whizzing and honking, and whistling mirrors just barely miss me.
Tired of dodging and darting, running and racing, I look to the place I last saw Him.

With joy, I realize that He was never far from me and my foolish ways have not caused Him to turn away.
He looks with love to me now, and opens His arms to a wayward son.
In His embrace, I find peace as I cry for joy!

In my Father's arms, and in His house, I am safe!
Now, I am a Free Bear indeed!

Cristo Redentor...

It wasn't His mercy, although without it, my sentence is death with no reprieve.
It wasn't His justice. Although my youth cries out passionately for it, my wisdom is grateful for His mercy – His faithful promises to forget.
It wasn't His blessings, although my life is sweeter for all of them.
It was His single-minded Love that delivered His Son and me from darkness to light – from death to life.
It is His love and the one commandment that delivers all others.
It was His Love, without which my Bible would have empty pages.
FATHER, IT IS my Brother that is your symbol.
It is His birth and shed blood that we call Your Greatest BLESSING. He is Your GIFT!

My heart is your resurrection throne.
Happy Birthday!

My "Not So Accidental Blessing"

Who knew that a walk through the meadow would reveal the treasure of my lifetime?
Not wild turkeys, or pheasant…or rabbits on the run…
No wild butterflies to be tamed, or eagles perched on high – diving from cliffs above the clouds.
No bees making buzz-type sounds, or humming birds pretending to be bees to trumpet lilies.
No silent winds running quickly across plains of grass with a disappearing flight path as blades of grass lay down and are resurrected.
My treasure was one blessed day in summer that gave birth to a new life and a new expression of loving.

Who knew that travels through marvels of the world would reveal the treasure of my lifetime?
Not fast-moving transit buses or subways that arrived at the future ahead of schedule….
No fast-growing money trees with bunches of bills to hamper inflation, and catch-up with COLA.
No politicians making honest-TTT a platform, that even angels would be deceived by.
No "Up with People" rainbow complexions with inset jewels of blue, brown and black.
In the end, there was a new day and a new feeling of hope when I watched my child grow into wisdom and grace.

Who knew that wearing clothes called "comfortable in my skin" could reveal the treasures of my lifetime?
Not a rapid ascent through the ranks as a fair-haired boy, or golden child.
No shiny cars to signal the arrival at success, or a new house in the "Jones' Neighborhood."
No "suits" making "back slapping"; or "politically correct"; and even God sound like part of "The Secret."
No feelings moving quietly through the corporate ghetto like waves of love and peace, to quiet the masses for the minute.
In the end, it wasn't the job, but the chance to fulfill fatherhood, brotherhood and friendship in full measure that was the treasure.

Continued…

Who knew that you, my accidental blessing, were no accident at all?
Who knew that planting a single seed in the center of a meadow could cause an orchard to grow?
Who knew that so many unsuspecting clouds would target the seeds over seasons for watering?
Who knew that I would recognize His work in you, because of the fruit you bore?
Who knew the harvest was not mine, but my "not so accidental" blessing was YOU?
Who knew?

One Grain of Sand...

When I am angry because Dad won't let me have my way,

I say...
I think I'll take the one grain of sand that represents me
and leave the beach...
Surely, it was me that held the ocean back and kept the tides in check.
If I hadn't been here, what would the plan have been? Chaos, I'm sure.
I think I'll make mention of these facts and see what He says.

Dad says...
My arrogant, willful child - you can have your way. It is your choice.
I love you... and recognize you from every other grain of sand on the beach.
You are special to Me - my plan includes you.
But, you must choose to be part of it.
In the plan, you will be perfected.
Listen for my voice and you will know your place.

I say...
Silly me, I was His special grain of sand all along.
He knows me and I know Him.
I have grown wiser as I await His replies.
I know now that He knows ALL.
And most of all, He knows and loves me.
If I left, He would miss me and I Him.
I'll wait until I can leave on better terms.
When and if I go, I'll be taking Him and the **peace** of His beach with me.

Dad, thanks for making me your favorite.

Heart's Work...

Loving Me is like recalibrating the meaning of Eifel-High and Mount Everest, as foothills in comparisons to My heavenly elevation...as My ways are not yours.
The ascent is never possible even with warrior's stamina, without My strength.
It's heart's work and I make no promises that the world will make it easy – so persevere.

Loving Me is NOT getting to the oasis without crossing the desert.
There will be no cooling waters or reclining on beds of shaded grass without first braving the heat or having rough surfaces polished smooth by blowing sand – thrown by My hand.
These trials, you must endure for a place of repose in the heart's oasis.

Loving Me is NOT going down into the valley without descending through narrow mountain passages.
There will be no gradual grades that channel waters to the river for splashing without reaching the precipice that seemed unreachable or building bridges.
The heights are preludes to the down-sides and the banks to streams of the heart awaiting.

Loving Me is NOT embracing unspeakable joy without realizing the path through pain that I have traveled.
There can be no laughter that echoes deep within your spirit without rejecting the intimate parts of fear, and the losing side of a natural life.
The hurt is the prelude to the healing that fills voids and promises a heart's foundation for a GREATER Love.

Loving Me is NOT aspiring to peace without preparation for the warrior's battle to test your mettle.
It will not come until you wield My swift sword and your parts hold My armor to rebuff the enemy's attack.

Continued...

Your battle armed with my gift and grace, is not won as you sit idle
 on the battlements, but requires work on the battlefield, 'though
 the outcome is foretold.
Loving Me is NOT demanding prosperity without the cost.
There will be no freeloads that show how you have been faithful
 without first proving that the Words of My first fruit are learned
 and not spoken.
It's heart work in the world and there are no promises that it will be
 easy – so persevere.

Loving Me is NOT wanting the reward of the seeds without due
 seasons of time 'til harvest.
The grapes will remain on pruned vines until they are too heavy to
 stay aloft - until the waiting Spirit shakes them, and the branches
 release them to My Hand.
They belong to me
Seeds released, will grow new fruit in fertile places of the heart that I
 picked long before time.

Loving Me will help you not to grow faint.
As you grow, you will be a mountain climber and a strong warrior –
 the summit and the outcomes are assured.
You were and are my harvest, and always My child.
Loving you is a *price paid*. You were lost, but I knew the hairs of your
 head, and called your name in what appeared a wilderness to
 you. My grace is sufficient.

Loving Me is the act of loving one another as I have
 loved you.
It is heart's work, and though my load is light the
 journey will not be easy – so persevere.
Endure knowing that Loving Me ripens your fruit and
 delivers your heart to My hand.

When the Well Runs Dry...

The days of tossing rocks from high above into the well's deep dark water have ended.
Rattles and ricochets echo back the message, "The well is dry."
Now, only the souls of departed droplets inhabit this barren place.
The sounds reminisce of what used to be while awaiting rebirth.
'til the well is renewed; I am alone in this my "Dark Night of the Soul."
Once, I looked down to levels I thought I would never know.
I now find my soul is filled with despair and loneliness as empty as this dark place.
I abide in a hollow place at the well's bottom where no light dares descend.
I hold desperately onto the last threads of hope and a promise remembered for this time.
If you believe in your heart and say...you will be saved.
"Prepare for an end and more emptiness to fill your vacuum...," the darkness exhorts.
"You are alone, and no one knows of your pain, or cares for you. Surrender and I will hold you."
I searched furtively for that last thread that would be a rope to lift me out.
None materialized, but a single ray of light pierced the darkness and a familiar voice called my name.
It was surely the voice in the desert and the one heard on the road to Damascus that echoed now in this place.
"Father is preparing this place for His Son's homecoming.
He will inhabit this empty place with fullness and light.
The voices will sing praises to salvation – joy and peace.
Do not believe what you have been told here.
They are lies for there is only One Truth.
The Savior is nigh. Faint not. Do not despair! Prepare!"

Fallen Petals...

Yesterday, the petals of a glorious flower fell to the earthen floor.
Today, they lie motionless beside the feathers of a flightless eagle.
It is here that the stories of two individuals merge.
She was a beauty and all the rage. He was a force of the air.
But that was yesterday.
Her blossom once thrust skyward to embrace the sun's rays.
But today, she no longer boasts the freshness of youth.
Her petals have now wilted beneath the onslaught of rain and life's short season.
The accolades she once embraced are now crushed between leaves of a book.
'Though still beautiful, she is an aged facsimile of the flower she once was.
For her, time, experience and knowledge have faded the blush of naïve youth and beauty.
He was a mighty eagle that once soared alone in his airy domain.
He needed no one while on flights to survey his kingdom from the highest heights.
His voice could be heard for miles through canyons and inspired fear and respect.
Today he has surrendered his lofty perch – minus his feathers he is flightless.
Now he can only stare up at mountain peaks that he once commanded and called home.
The places of his youth are now out of reach and powerful claws now hold him only to earth.
In earlier days, he admired a special blossom far below and she watched him soar without limits.
But now, his feathers and her petals are bound to a new reality.
This aged blossom and a flightless warrior now share a world together.
Screaming his fiercest battle cry to the heavens, as only the bravest of eagles can, he demands a reunion with windy flight and a return to his mountain peak.
And she in wilting sorrow and tethered to dying roots, begs for a new life – the rebirth of her petals and bright colors.
But ALAS, the seasons have changed again and again, and their pleadings go unanswered.
Time and time again, bring resignation and final surrender of wishes to the inevitable.
Both now give up hope of a return to the past, but not memories of what once was dear.

Continued...

She recollects the fresh newness of earthly beauty.
He still feels the rush of springing into the air from cloud covered peaks.
But never is the wilted flower returned anew to blossom, nor is a single feather reunited on the wing.

Together, they are transformed.
Both are lost to the past and introduced to change that brings new life.
The lesson is difficult, especially since yesterday was familiar and comfortable.
Today, yesterday is squandered and tomorrow is filled with expectations of new hope of a new type of life.

They are forever changed.

Suicide...

I've been in tunnels dark and wells too deep to fathom...
Sounds around, deafened me with whispers of my fears.
And when light finally made its way to me...years had passed.
Mirrors surrounded me reflecting the inner visions of my anguish...
Recordings of my childhood, my manhood, and all my yesterdays looped continually.
The haunting voices of a ghostly chorus sang my pain and repeated in dissonance – "Hopeless!"
My fear replanted a dead crop nearer to my heart to smother any chance of recovery.
I screamed for help through clenched teeth and fists and cried out for revival.
In my most desperate moment, when no ear could hear me, You answered my cry.
You spoke my name for salvation – my heart heard your voice and embraced a new life.
The night has almost ended, and the promise of recovery is coming, if I can only last that long.

Lesson Five

Keeping Family History...

The history of a family is seldom written..., but is shared across the dining room table, or in the kitchen, or on the front porch when the summer heat makes the house too hot to handle.

Up and down south, the "oral tradition" of passing history from generation to generation happened on the swing, sitting on the steps, watching the children play in the street under city streetlights, in front of the drug store over checker boards... or under the shade tree in the yard. But wherever, it seems to be the genetic inheritance that matriarchs remain to recount the stories, expand on the "legends" or simply to describe the lineage – no simple tasks.

Today, many of the matriarchs are gone and there's no one to pass on the legacy. For this, I am deeply saddened and make a small contribution here by just describing how Ruby would handle this, if she still lived.

The stories were told so frequently that her stories became my stories...our stories, almost like we lived them. And after a while, it seems that I was carried through the cotton fields or ran ahead of the dogs to freedom. It's our story, and it's personal, so I guess it is my story. I will tell it.

Sanguine Reminders

I repeat your question to myself and the answer to "Why I write," changes through the years.

In the recent years, it has shown itself to be a surgical instrument that opens my wounds for closer inspection – to remove forgotten remnants of explosive admonitions that could have destroyed me but have strengthened the most sensitive parts of my soul.

In times, when nothing deadened the hurt, it has been a balm to sooth the burning pain of warnings gone unheeded – "If you can't stand the heat, get out of the kitchen."

Then more recently, it has been a rough stone that sloughs away scar tissue to reveal new skin.
And sometimes, it is the filter that turns feelings into prayer – poetry from me to God, or stanzas that apologize and explain my feelings.

In the end, it is a sanguine reminder of how precious today really is, and how gracious God has been to leave me here to experience this moment.

Reflection on "Sanguine Reminders"

Folks ask me why I write. I ask myself the same question. It's not because I am a Hemingway, or Frost, or even some not so well-known local talent.

I write because, I believe that everyone has a story to tell. Everyone has something to say – to convey to the world a legacy that evaporates if not captured.

My story lives between the punctuation marks on each of these pages, and between the horizons of my first and last experiences – from sunrises to new moons – incognito and intermingled with the lives of others.

I write in hopes that my lines when read will live in the hearts of those I leave behind – that I might be remembered and live beyond my years.

My essence is here as a sanguine reminder that my life meant something to someone besides me – maybe.

Only Unique

I'd a thought that being simple would make me blend in, if I didn't know better.
But, it doesn't mean I won't stand out when surrounded by *boring, placid, or plain at best*...
There's no ignoring a lone sunflower on a grassy knoll.

I'd a thought the sun was just a near star waiting for *"black holedom,"* if I didn't know better.
But isn't it really an alarm clock for flowers napping between *blossom* and *bloom*.
There's no sleeping, when high leafy canopies get holey for its rays to shine through.

I'd a thought the moon was just hanging out to follow me home, if I didn't know better.
But it's a magic candle for igniting sparkle in the eyes of young lovers who hide in the dark.
There's no escaping, when "John Law" uses it as a flashlight and says, "Git on Home."

I'd a thought that being *me* would have been one of many choices, if I didn't know better.
But there's really no choice at all.
The skin I'm in is all I've got – no other birthday suits fit me better.

I'd a thought being *unique* would give me something to smile about, if I didn't know better.
There's still no one to talk to, being me.

I'll have to go searching, when the only other Dinosaur must have moved to someplace warmer.

I'd a thought that "lonely" was a different word
But now I know better...
It's not always such a good thing when *'unique" is* the word I write instead of *"by myself"*

Continued...

There's no hiding when the last monarch is a petal for the only tulip – the last flower in the vase and it means I'm by myself.
I'd a thought things would be different...
But in the end, it's just me...

Lesson Six -> Not Working...

Dealing with you in relationship..., I am trying to:

1. Be good → not working
2. Not think about you all the time → not working
3. Keep you out of my dreams so I can sleep → not working
4. Remember that I'm a role model and repeat #1 → not working
5. Be patient and not be pushy → not working
6. Not be upset when you can't spend time with me → really not working
7. Understand that you may still be in love with the other guy and repeat #5 above →definitely not working.
8. Wait for you to come to me so that I won't be perceived as not #5...whatever... → absolutely, positively not working.
9. Be happy regardless of how miserable I feel and not bring the world down with me → positively, absolutely not working.
10. Not feel my pulse racing when you're around → not working.
11. Stay busy so I won't feel like I'm missing something by not seeing you---→ nope, not working.
12. Not to want to punch my friends for calling to ask who you are...→ again really? Nope, really not working.

Okay,
so what do you want me to do with 12 really not working concepts?
What...?
Oh...HELL NO!
That's never gonna work!!!

My Dream Has a Name

When I behold my dream, her smile as radiant as a near star warms me.
Darkness crawls to caves and cowers in the shadows, as my dream appears.

When I hear the voice of my dream, the ocean roars in my ears.
The wind whispers things I cannot repeat, as my dream speaks

When I kiss my dream, no moment is more treasured, or surreal.
Ripe cherries call out in chorus begging to color and spread sweetness on her lips, before our lips meet.

When my dream is with me, she is like a fantasy.
Our arms and thoughts embrace like honey and tea blend to satisfy my abiding thirst.

My dream has a name, but I sing it only as a love song to her waiting ear.
In her eyes, I see the best of me and the goodness of a lifetime.

When I call to my dream, her name summons a beauty swiftly to the mist's edge of repose.
It is her that I see and recognize when my eyes open to an angel resting in slumber.

When I reach out to touch my dream, it is a noble heart that I find.
I reach out for a hand to guide me, and quickly find our fingers entwined.
My Dream has your name; she shares your smile; and she has captured my heart.
My dream is a fetching hunter and I am her happy prey.

LOST and FOUND...

When We Met...
I LOST all control, as your sweet spirit ruled my mind's eyes... and
My heart's desire was to be in your arms...since
I wasn't thinking... about memories, past pains and fading heartbeats...as
I longed to feel your eyelashes flutter against my cheek...on journeys to my
 lips...where they
Would languish for long moments to still my voice...and
Make my dreams come true...

Last Night...
I felt the heat of your thigh as you moved into me while we danced slow and
 sweaty, and
Like drops of water vaporizing on hot flat irons, my blood boiled...as
Hot coals rested in my loins with no promise of air conditioners for respite...you
 and
Your softness pushed logic from my mind as I battled against loss of all hope and
 control...and I
Looked to the night stars, wondering how I could entertain the idea of leaving....
 when
All my thoughts were of moist warmness and being into you...

This Morning
Sleep has not cooled the flames of passion as light peers through parted
 curtains...and
Your hands move the hairs on my chest, like oceans of wheat on a 40-acre
 field...as
Fingers play – as if to shake wheat from mature stalks...and
Each rests against its neighbor - beneath the gentle pressures of the wind - your
 breath...as
Your lips tarry like a violin's bow, pulling strings in my groin to an already
 crowded throat.

Now My Love...
The smell of your flesh has fanned and trained my
 flames of passion to be only yours.
It is what I remember above all...next to your taste –
 sweet lingering salt and honey.
A life-long addiction to "The One & the Only"
My heart, my mind and my words are my only gifts for
 love, and loyalty, NOW that I have FOUND you.

Tomorrow
I will find a way to tell you of love anew...
I will wake and know that I have found love...and
I will search for you and know that your smile has found
    its way to my cheek...so...
I will live knowing that I have found love, as your lips
    search for mine...and
I will take joy in knowing that our love is testimony to all
    that is good.

Yesterday's Tomorrows...
Were just out of view...where
My heart and I have waited for you, longed for your
    return, and loved you with this and every next
    breath.

The KISS

A soft and tender caress tethered to a heart looking
for lips of its own, as a call to love.
It has changed everything with a wave so powerful
that all else is of no consequence.
Of no import, the timing or place, a delicate balance
is maintained and lives between lips approaching.
All in the space, where a universe is created and
even a "Big Bang" is only a firecracker.
In the moment of a first kiss, nothing else matters.

Country Girl

You sang me a love song that only a country girl could sing. It was like collard greens, cornbread and okra, on a Sunday after church.
You sang a straight talk refrain.
You whispered words in a husky voice when only I could hear. You're my kinda country with no frills, no regrets and no fear.
You deserve a song as a reminder of all the places you've never gone. So I'll write your lyrics to a simple harmony and I'll sing you my simple song.
It'll say, "You came softly to my life – I'll never be the same. My words of love had no meaning 'til I learned to sing your name."

You sang me a love song that only a country girl sings.
Like snug fitting' denim with no pretense in your walk, you said how you feel – you acted like you talk.
Your words were 'bout being real, not denying what used to be.
You're my kinda country, with genuine lovin' – your sweets for only me.
You deserve a love song as a reminder of all the mountains you've never climbed.
So I'll write your lyrics to a simple harmony and I'll sing you my simple song.
It'll say, "You came softly to my life – I'll never be the same. My words of love had no meaning 'til I learned to sing your name."

You sang me a love song that only my country girl could sing. Like a flower in the desert, you made me feel like Spring.
Your lovin' was so fresh and my heart had all your attention. You gave me peace and joy and showed me life's new dimension.
You deserve a song as a reminder of where you've gone. I'll write your lyrics to a simple harmony and I'll sing 'bout our simple love song.
It'll say, you came softly to my life and I'm not the same.
It'll say my words of love had no meaning 'til I learned to say your name.
So, I'll write your lyrics for steel guitar with a harmony of twang... I'll sing it in the key of country to embrace your name.

Precautionary Measures...

Imitations never work like the real thing.

There will be NO WARNING, when Reality sets-in – "Guard your heart from pretenders."
Short hours rush away when passion
makes a pretense of love.

Demands are just part of the deal for imitations.
But then, the reality is that MOST things don't last forever...
The challenge is how to make it last when there are ONLY
brief hurried moments and the clock won't stop ticking.
There will be NO WARNING, when Reality returns.

Stolen moments cannot mask the disappointment when
there's really nothing left to say but "See you soon.".
It's all about the moment, so why do we hang on?
This is especially true, when the feelings and words
have temporary stamped all over them, for two to read...
There's Nothing left to say when the last line of day is "NSA."
"Guard your heart from vain lies that want to be truth."

There will be NO WARNING, when Reality is a present shadow.
The times alternate between miniature explosions of gas
vapors, open flames and pleadings on rug-burned knees.
The only constants are matches to ignite pitied souls and the lust
that waits anxiously beneath the sheets for promised heat.
With "always demands" and less rendezvous as professions
of love walk to the door for good, bad, or nevermore. So
guard your heart.

Pretense looks like wood chips without glue to bind them – poor imitations of boards, or used-to-be trees. Like lies frequently repeated and Xeroxed to resemble truth, or change the complexion, or the feelings of deceit.
Soon, time will be up and there'll be nothing left, but ashes and cinders to remind us of the short time we once had.

In My Skin...

Who am I to say...

The world seeks out opportunities to put tape measures, and yard sticks, and calipers on judgment, thoughts and actions of every microbe. But, I am below the radar and ignore all attempts to be measured and managed. I reject the borders and fences that attempt to contain the spirit of the wild man that lurks within. I push back and push down doors, and reject rules that tell me who to be in my private times and publicly. But they are all private times in my mind. There is a statute of limitations on occupancy – only me in my mind and by my standards.

Only the experts know where to be or how to stand for something, or nothing, or everything they think important. I think not! I determine the stature of the man I am. I stand tall when others sit quietly, and sit in silence when the world screams for attention. I know the limits of my skin and reject any attempts to stretch my confinement to hold more than just me. I remain the only inhabitant of my skin and the sole proprietor of the reflection in the mirror...down to the marrow – I continue to be the owner. Not you, but me.

The measure of this man is against standards that I erect on door frames and along mountain trails – on sequoias that were here before the rules of your modern society.

Continued...

I am determined to spend a lifetime in my own head and about the same amount of time in my own birthday suit. I will be the body mechanic for me, and no one else will invade this space. Like everyone else, I will be running out of time and have no time to live someone else's life or lie.
So who am I to say that you can't make decisions about my heart, my head or my feelings? Quite simply, IT'S ALL ABOUT ME!

Who I am, is a decision by me that's not subject to discussion, or your approval. GET USED TO IT!

What makes you think...

A country western Falling Outta Love song...

You must not love me or care for me - to misuse me and treat me the way you do...
This sounds like a country western "Fallin' Outta Love Song" don't it?
When did, "Sorry about that..." constitute an apology?
When did not calling and leaving me stranded - waiting for you, equal having a good time?
What makes you think that "Don't take it personal..." takes the pain out of "I think it's time we said so long..."
The sad part is, that when all the tears have dried, I still think "If wishes made it so, you'd be with me.
But wishes don't, and you're not..."
And maybe you think that "Get a life..." is the best way to say "Goodbye!"
Well, I have and now it's my turn, when your new love is just like you.
Maybe now you'll understand why your harvest looks just like the seeds you've planted.
But, I can't bring myself to sing this same song to you.
So I'm singing a song, I've just written.
Mine is a new song... "What makes you think, I forgive you? But I do."
This sounds like a country western "Ready For a New Love" song, don't it?

"Planting Orchards"

A Delicious Apple from a single tree in the orchard transplanted half the world away is still a delicious apple. The beauty of this model is that the sweetness of the fruit remains the same and is not diminished by distance.

The new orchard from this apple is connected. In life, we share ideas that do not lose their brilliance with repeated telling, as long as they are repeated faithfully. Told around the world, they remain just as brilliant and as true.

As family, we are not limited by location or distance, but remain part of the whole. The sweetness of love is not diminished. The new family and old are connected. This is spiritual fruit.

Foolishness

In younger days, I believed there was more than enough time to make mistakes and to recover for a GREAT finish in later years. So, I played with jewels as if they were marbles, and on occasion lost them in tall grass and high weeds. Now, with improved vision, I've rediscovered them. It's as if they were awaiting my return.

Then perfected foolishness called witty, was an art form, and later I believed foolishness a waste. But, now that I have rediscovered those misplaced jewels in dense vegetation and have come full circle to my now, at the end. I look at earlier beginnings and I also understand that foolishness is sometimes a yardstick for wisdom and greater appreciation for simple truths when youth has withered, and life has blossomed.

Honey…

I am slain and revived by words…
And have found new meaning as I talk, waxing eloquent and extolling the virtues of you…

In words, passion is captured for today and for an eternity to remind the world
Of what we once had on wordless encounters.

Endings, punctuated with kisses have changed my path…
To a keeper of sweet juicy fruits called…
Your lips…, your smiles, your taste…
More than words.

Now I am a canner, to capture forever, your sweet nectar…
All mine…, Honey.

When Dreams May End…

Even though thoughts of you warm my bed and loins,
I must push away the day to remain with you.

And I know that you wait there…,
in surreal beauty for my speedy return.

'Tho time has stopped - eternal light beckons me "Come!"
As my time here is now complete.

Smiling Angel friends walk beside, and escort me weightless, to a place of dreams, where you are waiting, to welcome me home.

Won Sentence e-mail

The words "I Love You" have battled and won
Against the persistence of the "Delete" key
And managed to enter a void to find their way to your eyes
A "won sentence" email that survived
To fight its way back to me...
Preceded by "RE:..." and
Accompanied by "...you too Baby."

Preamble to Life

Today we walked and talked about a love for words...
Dropped like bread crumbs along the path...to follow
They were nuance and innuendo...life and breath
Power and heat..., "our now and your tomorrows"
The movement from hot to cold and daybreak to dusk...
Our conversations...painted allusions...life metaphors
More than naught, and fond memories for today...
As the rain drenched the path, the leaves,
You and me... and made us a rainbow ending.

Fan Male...

I am not looking for a fan club of more than one
As your rock star, I will only perform behind your walls
On your stage, your dance floors and your stairs...
I will sing for an audience of one, with unlimited encores...to...you

Familiar...

Puzzles are made to forms... fitting pictures and show...

That when the pieces go unfit, a reciprocating saw is not the answer...

And dismantling pain, a pause for the cause – a Dark Chocolate fix is not the answer...

But then I have been known to be happily wrong...
A reciprocating saw is not the answer...,
But chocolate may be...

No Sculpting Love...

The heat of the dance has softened you to me...
And twisted me in memory of more subtle days...
And molded a molten me to be closer...inseparable...

Fit together our bodies our minds in unison...
Our hearts beat connected...
Our spirits committed...

All without resorting to sledge and chisel...

Paradise Awaiting

When your soft arms open wide to embrace me
That is kissing in French you know
I will feel the warmth of you against my chest
So soft and warm, a pillow for my heady thoughts
And memories by my arms of your shoulders and waist
My legs will be entangled with yours in competitions I gladly lose
Pouty Lips wanting to clutch yours will still trembling as
My nose beneath your chin, pushes into the hollows of your neck
Searching past your cheeks to earlobes ready for whispered secrets of love

Continued...

That will warm and flush when all is said and done, knowing that paradise is waiting
As my arms open wide to embrace you –" embrassment"
That's to be kissing you in French, you know
And I'll thank God for "Paradise Found" and never more lost...

Almost Mistaken Identity...

I have defrocked a thousand rose blossoms and
Placed the petals of yellow, pink, and red
On a come-hither bed to invite you
Into a delicious potpourri of smells
That reminded me of our intimate
Times together, only to find you
Hiding quietly and waiting
For me to realize that you
Are the most beautiful rose
To lay beside me for blissful repose...

"I AM" to a Woodland Queen

Sweet Woodland Queen, you make me smile as you share me with the world.
I am flattered and whatever good you see and want, and perhaps need me to be.
Your descriptions are what they are, as long as I am your Woodland King.
Express me to others in the glade ANY Way you choose...to foxes, birds and the like.
For my love to you and for you, is your creation and a mirrored image of your heart.
My love for your seeing, feeling, and embracing – a blessing for your gratitude.
My love from you and of you is a blessing, a gift, and a stillness within.
I AM will hold you closer than a reflection to be in the joy you share with the world..., and sometimes me.

Color Palettes on the Hillside

I know 'perfect' when spring, summer and fall colors drape across hillsides.
Something deep within me says that this is as good as it gets, as I pray this season never ends, and that the Perfect Painter never stops creating the hillside pictures for my pleasures and His. But the gesso of winter wipes away all traces and perfection, and however improbable, begins again – painting a new and perfect picture on the hills framed by my window.
I know perfect when I see it and my years chronicle 'perfect' uniquely.

Daydreamer

You ask, when do I find time to work when daydreams of you are my preoccupation?
With laughter, I respond "How could it be otherwise…, when clearly the most important thing in my world is you…,
Pink, Red and Green, My Yellow Rose, My Queen…"
As you tell my heart that you love me "Still"

You ask, when do I find time to work when daydreams of you are my preoccupation?
I work hard, and very fast so that time between stanzas will be short, as I usher you into my conscious hours
as a prelude to sleeping with visions of you on a rose petal bed inside my head
As you whisper that you love me "Still"

You ask, when do I find time to work when daydreams of you are my preoccupation?
I work to have time to sit and write you love poems whenever my mind and heart think about your lips,
your arms, your beautiful hands, and every part of you…, and especially your mouth
As you murmur that you love me "Still"

You ask, if I find time to work when daydreams of you should be my preoccupation?

With a smile I respond, I have traced your mouth with each uttered syllable and now
I know their every movement by heart...for every repetition
As you quietly proclaim that it is "ME that you love...Still and Always"

Now you have answered my question and I will put daydreams aside and reach out for you.
Sleep love and dream of me...

Heart's Lost and Found

My heart smiles now that you have claimed it from the lost and found...
to be your pillow, the cushion for your beautiful crown...

I am honored to have held your hand...
no plan sweeter that I might smell my perfect flower through nighttime hours...

My lips recollect your smile across the restaurants "a bisque..."
as if not even an hour has passed since I held you near.

Take my love to bed with you and give it a home...
since you have altered it forever to be only yours.

Put our hearts together and they will smile in ways passion has yet to imagine.

Sharing Your Life...

Breathe for me...deeply
And taste the air that fills your lungs...
That will one day make its way to me...
Replenished somewhat with oxygen and scented of life...
I will pull it into my chest,
Too, to be kissed and blessed by what you have left for me...
Breathe deeply FOR me.
And I will breathe deeply OF you...
I will taste you in every part of me

On-Time Arrival...

The pixeled "X's" and "O's" leap from the screens at the end of
    sweet musings...
Accompanied by soundbites that affect my phone...Taaaa
    Daaaaahhhh!!!
TO tease me mercilessly, knowing that the winged miles
    separating us are heartless
Refusing to let your moist kisses refresh my lips or caress the
    lobes of my ears.

Relent I beg you... That you not worsen the situation by amplifying
    my passions
With multiplied XXOOs and XXXOOO...with lipstick impressions
    persuading a jealous me
That the screen on your side of my hand has had the pleasure
Of Feeling your lips to send that enticing redness and
    "Swaaaaaahs" sound pieces...

Not surrendering I reach out with "Hugggs and Kisses" finishing
    my pleas... "Hurry!!!"
Having embraced the phone... to embed my growing passions and
    southern heat
I now wait at the restaurant to see you move through the airline
    doorway...
With real redness spread around the whiteness of ready sentinels

As your approach, with each step, signals your desire to fulfill the
    20 "XXXX" promises
Of yesterday... and you know that I have kept these as ready
    coupons
For the reality of your lips and my hugs to hold you captive
XXXX OOOO XXXX OOOO Ahhhh!

Conspiracy Not to Love...

I never once conspired to love you but ran fleet of foot from the scene of my weakness.

But unawares, you found perfect moments sans pretense and caught me off guard.

I stumbled and fell for all of my life as you've held me captive - a cared for prisoner with no desire to escape...

Today, I remember deep longings as Black Boys in Passing shouted..." Awwww, go on and Kiss her..."

So now, there's no getting up to run from your bed, but so smitten by you, I've fallen further..., entangled, entwined, enraptured, into love.

And after short months of minutes and seconds, I stand briefly to close the door on my gilded cage and lock myself within your outstretched arms.

I never once conspired to love you, but I run now to my weakness - your sweetest embrace.

Park Dancing...

Do you remember a Saturday morning
of soulful tunes and joyous beads of sweat?
We danced, not caring if the world watched,
wanted to join in or mocked my lack of rhythm.
We heard nothing but the music and each other's laughter.
We were park dancing and the grounds were
off limits to the world - giving entry only
to Frankie Beverly, the "Temps," or the Four Tops.
The baseball field was transformed into
a dusty ballroom floor that marked
our steps for others to follow after we were gone.
The walls of this make-believe space
moved out in retreat from our
wild gyrations and swings.
The floor was alive and supported our
movements and whims.
The grass rebounded to our jumps and tilted to our slides.
Our park dancing created a world all ours
and none could enter while the music played.
Park dancing is what we'd never dared
before that night's curtain had fallen
to set the moon's mood.
Never park dancing in the daylight until
then...and never since.
Come again into my arms
with your laughter and your disbelief
to watch the clouds above
move to our rhythm.
We should go park dancing once more.

by Ronald Montgomery

Angels I must have seen...

Baby memories ...
So peacefully she sleeps – remembering I'm sure the things I've long forgotten.
She knows the things I long to recall.
Oh the things, you must have seen and still remember.

The wonder and awe of all you've known,
but will soon forget.
I suspect that you still see the faces of angels and hear the voice of God.
With your eyes open to the world, you strain to see heaven just out of view.

Unfortunately, you will not gain your voice soon enough
To tell us of God's wonder and the angels on high....
Oh the things, you must have seen and still remember.

The wonder and awe of all you've known,
but will soon forget.
But even as your memories fade, some inklings will stir at the sound of mama's voice.

It will be heaven's chorus, and her touch will be a reminder of angel's wings and God's embrace.
No wonder you smile so when she kisses those chubby cheeks...

You smile and flash that toothless grin...
Oh the things, you must have seen and still remember.

The wonder and awe of all you've known,
but will soon forget.
You'll only have to wait a lifetime to be reminded...
But only, when God calls your name the last time.
Now, go to sleep and remember while you can.
Shortly, you will miss the memories just out of recollection, and you will suspect, but never quite
know why you recognize God's voice when He speaks to your spirit.

Oh the things, you must have seen and still remember.
The wonder and awe of all you've known,
and will one day recall.

Reflection on "Angels I must have seen..."

There is a poem by Robert Fulghum entitled "All I Really Need to Know I learned in Kindergarten." The premise is that children pick up on a basic set of rules that would do us all good to remember, but we conveniently forget.

Children are also gifted with unbridled curiosity, creativity, insight, simplicity and moral compasses that many adults have lost, or conveniently misplaced.

I envy the children, especially when I hear their simple responses to complex questions. They have answers that must surely have come from heaven. Angels and God must still be speaking to them.

I believe that on some level, they can still hear His voice and the voices of angels that accompany them.

Following what we believe is a mandate, we work on grounding them in this world. They are encouraged, it seems, to lose the sense of wonder when we should be helping them to hold onto it.

I am working on regaining this ability. I'll know when I've arrived because I will be on the same level with my grandchildren. They will smile at me and we will talk together - *Spirit to Spirit*.

It was Never Love...

... a misunderstanding between two fools

We've begun and ended...playing cat and mouse
with prizes more tasty than cheesy morsels.
Our comings and goings punctuated
with adrenaline rushes of "free fall"
as we "stepped out" at 40,000 feet looking for more.
And thrilling though it seemed...
we pushed apart vowing...
"Never love."

Two bodies in transition,
we came together... hard.
Two atoms colliding and releasing
energy – devastating and potent –
like hot spots on near stars.
Self-proclaimed experts of love,
we showered the blackness behind closed eyelids
with pyrotechnics of exploding dwarf galaxies.
These orgasmic experiences moved
us in our words to the corner of "Friendship"
but never "Love."

We uttered words and shaded phrases,
hinted and alluded, and pushed from without the envelope
that held within true meanings.
And laughing, we courted
the cliff's edge beyond casual acquaintance,
knowing what lies beyond.
And swore the fall would only bend,
fragile feelings hidden from sight –
friendship fueled by passion.

It was a friendship, a game,
a play, but never "Love."

We viewed as spectators
emotions laid bare by life,
while lamenting the pain
and applauding small successes.
We hid in sunlight,
lied in darkness, ...never quite sure of our roles.

Continued...

And fueled by our convictions,
we saw what time alone could witness.

Feelings and caring – the sensitive side
of responsible and practical, were more than games,
and far more than friendship required...
They were signs on the marquis for
"Always in Love with You"

Who was she?

She was a flower in the desert.
Surrounded by cacti, dust and heat...,
She bloomed and blossomed and brought love into my life.

She stood straight and proud in a land of multicolored dullness.
She dwarfed the Eiffel Tower in her greatness and
shamed the Louvre
With her artfully wrought ebony features.

She created masterfully correct concepts, and was
More insightful than the greatest philosophers.
She had more plaited naps than Buddha.

She was the definition and true meaning of beauty.
She was the mold of greatness, the cast of proper,
The graduate of right, and she brought me joy.

Who was she?
Why *Love*, it was you.

by Ronald Montgomery

Almost Paradise... (Dementia)

Lost is the feeling now, since remembrance of what I left to be here escapes me. So here is where I am stopping for a brief time.
My recent "yesterdays" are lost, and a few moments have gone missing, or half remembered as I watched you knit from skeins and crochet from memory.

The edges of my mouth wrinkle at some recollection, since I know silently that the time for forgetting is almost gone.

Memories are scattered across the bed and almost cover the quilt patterns pulled together before your memories faded.

I remember now, when your face came into view, like sunshine captured between wrinkled hands that surely must be someone else's.
I see so many partial masterpieces scattered around.

I remember your nimble fingers that lost their way more and more as they rushed in syrupy motions to finish... and looked for completion before departing.

I remember at the end - just before you left me, you'd almost begun and finished your three-fingered glove for me.

And I remember that your hugs and kisses were the closest thing to paradise for me.

My faded memory almost recollects a polka dot dress stained with love's perfume..., and a wilted rose of a night never forgotten...but now a memory fainting in near woods.

My mind grasps at a child waiting to be held and caressed into a forgetfulness of a missed feeding..., a diaper now Dockers and loafers thrown into the corner.

After almost a lifetime of waiting, and Milton's loss and now my almost paradise found..., I feel like it's almost time to go home..., and almost time to let you go... and lose the glow between parted lids.

Continued...

Almost asleep now...so tired, but Almost Paradise coming into view...
    It's no recollection that I see you beside my son and daughter waiting... for me.

And I know NOW the end of forgetting has arrived.
    My paradise is found.

Perfect Vision after 50 Years...

In our early days, you were perfect and so was I.
Better eyesight wouldn't have been an improvement.
I didn't say I had 20/20 vision.
I just said it was perfect when it came to you.
My eyes saw every curve that made me want to reach
out and touch you...

In our middle days, we changed, and glasses were
sometimes needed to overlook the flaws.
Later in the relationship, we replaced the glasses with a microscope.
Every flaw was crisp and clear.
In our latter years, bifocals allowed us to see our own
mistakes from previous years as part of an eye test.

Today, when we blew out 50 candles on our
anniversary cake, my best vision returned.
Still, it's not 20/20, but it is perfect when I look at you.
My eyes again see all the curves that make me want to
reach out and caress your brow...

Lies

Reality arrives when my eyes open in the morning.
You and Your love are mine to own and possess.
My "Material Things Collection" measures my wealth.
Making love this time is the best experience of a lifetime.
I will take this moment with me when I depart this place.
Knowledge and logic explain all of this.
Science is the way..., and I am in control of my existence.
Alley Apples are not fertilizer.

Truth

We think too small and dream too little.
Goodness and beauty are wonderful things.
Beauty is far better than good looks.
Your opinions joined to mine won't buy a cup of coffee.
Drinking from the same cup will bring us closer together.
Every truth births a star in the heavens.
Stars equal the number the times I tell you I love you.
The truth is, "I love you..." even when the lights are on...
Another star has just appeared.

Wedding Dance...

He has given me YOU, 'though you may only be mine...to have -
To hold, a lease on love – a dance to spice my life this season...
To dance joyous for a time long enough to capture new...
These feelings with you, in forecast of ballroom memories...
Where we will dance together laughing, and
Cavorting to happy..., even when the music stops...
Let the songs play on, so our dance never ends...
"I will do a dance for you."

FATUOUS

Ahhh my Love.
She walks in grace, and creates repetitive newness in
every movement . . . never the same, but always
quite as beautiful as just a moment before, in an
aura that never changes . . . in actions all her
own . . . uncopiable, unaffected, and most unbelievable.

She speaks in the wind, with lips slightly parted
revealing mother of pearl whiteness, borrowed
from the folds of oyster shells, and that frame
each word in perfection.
So breezy is her voice.

She caresses my name and strokes, with a certain
gentleness, letters fortunate enough to form
words that find origin on her lips . . . and she
lulls my ears with breathy whispers of "Ahhh...."
She speaks to my heart.

She glances now and again from brooding brown
molasses pools fringed with down. She graces
the world with a single glance . . . but I so
fortunate . . . with countless looks and stolen glimpses.
Plants grow beneath her gaze, and I blossom in the
reflection of me, in the depths of her eyes.

Of obsidian carved, she is perfection wrought.
Never before would I have thought, that anywhere such
fairness could be.
Having found it, I am ecstatic that in moments of
passion, she calls me "Love."

Yesterday's Feast...

Give back my yesterday in place of today...
My heart is in need of the healing you
gave in stroking the thin wisps and balding locks...

Give me back my escape to a place
where your love fed me; your warmth comforted me; and your
bubbling laughter quenched my thirst.

I want that spot of heat in a cold wasteland
you gave me yesterday at our moveable feast.
Give me back yesterday in place of today.
It has set such a lofty goal that no day will ever match it.

Knowing this, what need do I have for another sunrise.
My moments of serenity in your world have ended.

I want that spot of heat in a cold wasteland
you gave me yesterday at our moveable feast
Please, give back my yesterday in place of today.

Smiles Reprise

My creative child emerged on a daily romp to the mall and down
    the hall
And I listened to the music and knew the muse within...
As I smiled once... then twice...and then once again...
How wonderful it felt when it reached from my nose
Through my joyous heart and my soul and down to my toes
It played for a time in wrinkles and creases that filled my face
And left it's impression in lines deepened by feelings from inner
    space
My lips knew the "happy" that coursed within...
To be blessed...and able to do it again and again
So now I rest content knowing that more than once I smiled
It was my joy...my smile was heaven sent

"Not Uniquely Yours…"

In your diary, I read words indelibly inked…
In relations past, and now I realize with sickened gut…
You've loved like this before…
Now I am not uniquely yours…

Many times over you've written down
Memorials to lovers to live forever
On pages, in dreams, as echoes, in
A life not hollow at all, but full – full to bursting
With "Befores…," "Thens…," "Untils…."
And "Nows" and I am not uniquely yours…

Not unique, I conclude, nor special, nor rare;
Invisible among so many; Yet vivid, vital, valuable as…?
Yet present in your Present?
Air to your every breath---
The one you love Today and a lover of you…

Is it me…?

"A Moist Inky Reply..."

A Reply to Not Uniquely Yours

Alas, you have read my letters...my books
And answered your own questions of
My constancy and I uniquely a lover of you
And have come away with a view of my history...
But not of today and not of you and me...

You must know this, ...
The ink on this page still smudges and runs fresh...
Telling of loving strokes and touches...of feather lightness...
And heavy...hearts full of emotion, longing and fresh...
The smell of lilacs and roses just picked today...
Mingled with inky smells fading...to new scribbles...

Dried flowers of my past have made me a lover...
Of beautiful bouquets, and you a sexy, sensuous creature...
Not diminished by what has passed, nor of ink dried...
Promises made and broken, and fulfilled in regret...
But eagerly, we wait for a tomorrow that none before you "have," nor ever will "be."

You are Unique among the many...
Where flowers in my garden have not your scent...
Nor are they attended as the last most beautiful bloom...
Gone are all, while you have blossomed for this season...
That I may love and be loved by you like no other for reasons...
Only God will ever really know.

It is you...!

Be Not Dismayed...

Be not dismayed, if your letters grow into replies for poetic gardens that yield more than daffodils...and feel better than furry caterpillars on the way to Monarch Butterflies...

This is the "more" that you will hopefully want to know, as your knowledge of our union grows...

Be not dismayed or surprised that there are things in my past that will disarm you, or make you love me despite your imaginings or make you push me away quickly, to gather your breath, or teary thoughts...

This is the "more," that we will want to feel, as the knowledge of our union grows...

Be not dismayed or surprised that I have thought your thoughts and kept them as mine in preparation for our next meeting when I will pick up scattered bouquets and arrange them anew on a bed where we will lie...

The "more" that we will discover when letters from me fill your love chests and grow into juicy poems for only you...

Be not dismayed that the words that speak of love to you are not new spellings or unique phrases.

Just know that their meanings are recreated daily in a sweet and beautiful you.

"Hallmark Lover"

I smile, at the words of Hallmark, wordsmith and other giants of cellophane, aluminum foil and colored papers, who capture our feelings and sandwich them within envelopes for you to hide in my shirts, socks and briefs.

They are just for me to discover on subway rides, winged TWA, or just before my tired head drifts down to a waiting pillow.

I smile with a sublime sense of warmth, knowing that your love finds new avenues of fresh inventiveness...with one word or a thousand...to raise my spirits to new heights and to say the things that reinforce our feelings of love for one another.

I smile knowing my "Hallmark Lover" is continually at work finding new ways to say "I love you. I miss you. I care!"

Ditto love!!! Me too.

LINT

Some might want to disconnect from the fabric of humanity. How does a thread disconnect from the fabric?
Can it pull itself free of the colorful fabric of humanity, to be separated?
Yes, perhaps so. For that disconnected thread, there is a name – "Lint."
But even lint gets connected to dust balls, or dryer filters.
Watch out. Here comes the trashcan.
I guess threads have a choice. Right?
Fabric or recycling bin...

Ticks in your Knickers...
(Anonymous Words of Wisdom)

When life gets difficult and unpredictable, put everything down, grab your pole and jus' go fishin'.

Write down your poetic lines and then put them away. When you return, more times than not, they will have organized themselves in amazing ways. Just pick up your pen and write.
All your creative thoughts and inklings need to be saved and not erased... Remember the delete key...? Forget it. Once the ideas escape from you, somebody else gets to write them down and say, "Mine..."
Last but not least, a bit of ancestral knowledge. Be careful in tall grass. Leopards and other large cats hunt there. And even worse you'll likely get ticks in your knickers.

Anonymous

Reflection:
These are wise sayings from an anonymous sage. After all, that is what sages do, but create wise sayings for us to pass on. That's the job description, right?

PS. Actually, I am "Anonymous." So now, these seeds of wisdom will be replanted, and my name will appear in the dictionary beside the definition. How do you think, I got to be a sage? I wrote the definition, that's how!

"IF This is Now... Now What?"

This is the NOW...Next Now...What NOW...that is an echo none want...

To hear, we talk, as we walk paths curving through wooded sanctuaries - reminiscing on future memories, of planned retrospectives after holiday dinners. Our "now...next now..." are punctuated by swishing nylon sweats and unheard electronics... Imaginary toc-toc, tic-tic, tic-toc – tech with one direction, swinging forward, "Rolex" unreadable, to and fro, advancing to the parking lot...15 minutes ahead in our future.
This is the NOW...Next Now...What NOW...that is an echo none can...

Here, the steps never retreat...as we discuss the times of today's war and bygone friends, as leaves of a *single season* float earthward on the path before us...while lonely *few* on outstretched branches, hold on for dear life..., but are forgotten by gold and crimson brothers who have surrendered - ignored in brown grass... These are the memories left behind, while some remain – "Care Bears" in toy chests and clipping like dried flowers on the coffee table. These are the "Nows" turned to yesterdays,...the "Nows" not remembered..., the "Nows" never forgotten...on bare branches...

As clouds advance, droplets signal a rainy future..., where this "Now" is punctuated by a soundless unreadable watch that knows nothing of a sure arrival of "wet" in our future. The here is now.

Surely, the talk of children...of pain...of joys - happy joys that point and lead the way to our "future storytelling" ...are in the past, as we point departing cars in the direction of tomorrow
This is the Next NOW...What Now... NOW What... Now is "Still Breathing..." Now what?

Singing ~~THE BLUES~~ Country Western

I guess I'd be singing the blues
If my cowboy boots and PBR buckle didn't give me away.
So I guess I'll be singing country western
Or blow my cover...

Messenger

I was always an angel...
Long before you pulled me to earth...I fell...
My feathers are now in the grass at my feet, ...
And my wings – now invisible...in love...
Continue to embrace and shield you
Do you see what you have done to me...?
I was always an angel...for you
When I fell to earth in love...
I fell for you...

Déjà ~~vu~~ Ear

Just because you can say that again, doesn't mean that I need to hear it again...

Back to the Beginning...

I'm back to the beginning where
I thought I'd never be
A Déjà vu of you and me
When discovery was
A question of what we'd be
To each other
A beginning that looks
Now like the end again...
Hello...It's me...

25 YEAR STALEMATE...

Our relationship is at a stalemate...
Your way or mine, 100% against 150% for...
And I will not be persuaded...
Happy Anniversary!

The Wink

Cypress leaves and sycamore bark of nearby trees have been taken captive by fall winds, lifting them in an eloquent dance just beyond my window. They float to what seem designated spots on the ground below – an earthy scarf floating down to caress and hide your nakedness from prying eyes, for a moment in time. Just as the eclipse is a blink of a nighttime eye winking at me from eternity.

I am winking back.

Anastomosis ERSATZ

If you want to be with me, just tweet me with 140 and a picture. Blog me a Letter...a communication beyond
You... Me.... Touching hands and lips for a life...

<Next Tweet> ...time
Meet me in the blogosphere for a relationship if you dare...
Reach out to me and touch my...

<Next Tweet> ... heart.
Please pass the potatoes...

<Next Tweet> Yummy! Thank you Love

Lost Stockings

Where have they gone...
Disappeared into pant legs and...
Crawled into sleeves
I've seen them hiding...
Never understanding why...
Five Black and 3 Whites...
And multi-colored stripes by the by...
Nestled in knickers, and pant legs...
a static relationship to be sure...
Socks with no match...
A Match with no mate...
What are they hiding from...?
Me?

AAAHHHH...!

I die in new knowledge and sudden peace as bedside audiences watch and I perform the last great feat In my time...

Forgiveness... Voila'

I Dared to Tell You...

I dared to admire you from a distance
Great enough to hide my heart
And you saw "Me"
Despite stealthy attempts at getting closer
I was blessed by your discerning spirit and good vision
And now I know that my shyness will be ignored
In favor of true feelings and honesty
Here I am..., I am yours.

by Ronald Montgomery

SURVIVOR... Not yet complete...A Reflection

REFLECTION: "I will find a way to write about them...," I tell my friends now, a decade later.

She was a beauty that he married during times when she graced the covers of Vogue and Mademoiselle. Now she is a "Survivor." The cancer had tried to ravish her body, and left her with missing parts and scars, but their love only enhanced her beauty. To him, she was the eternal queen and his passionflower.

To me, they were and are the models that restore my vision of love and caring. I knew the backstory, but they never knew this. I will keep this part secreted away, or at least the names and locations, but the story needs telling. There are about 3.6 billion men who are waiting to know what they should be aspiring to... "I will find a way to write about them...," I tell my friends.

I have never forgotten the night that he and I sat on the deck talking – listening to the waterfall in the background and drinking wine. Then his cell phone rang. She was calling to him from the bedroom. She told him to come.

I didn't hear it..., the conversation, that is. He repeated it gleefully..." I am waiting for you", she had said. Even as he told me, he took his wine and the stairs two at a time... In rapid ascent, he raced to her. I was truly impressed and for the first time, I knew what love looked like.

And for the first time, I knew sweet jealousy. I wanted..., and still want the same thing for me. "I will find a way to write about them...," I tell my friends.

Today, I practice leaping up the stairs, two and three at a time. I keep the phone charged, in preparation for running to her side. When My True Love calls, I will spring to the ready and fly through the air to reach her.

I am determined that I will find a way to write about them and to tell my friends.

From the Outside In

Snowflakes outside my window seem to be shouting
out permissions... for me to lie warm, beneath
comforters and duvet...

As a white blanket outside gives the world a chance
to rest pristine for a time...
A gesso to be glorified when the sun peeks through
reflecting brilliance from each flake...

And finally, to Spring up rejuvenated when watery angel
feathers escape back to heaven and...
Waters, green sprouts and rainbow's flowers...

Today, I will love it from the inside, looking out...
What a wondrous sight...from the inside.

A Simple "XOXO" Prayer

I will take time and send out a prayer for my favorite
person.

You will feel warm and love will spread in your chest
knowing that He...our Dad...heard my prayer and
sent you an extra measure of "Hugs and Kisses" not
because I asked Him, but because they were already
on the way. He just liked knowing I thought enough
of you to pray.

Smiles. Today, will be a really good day.
You just don't know it yet..., or do you? -)

XOXO

Rejoice

If you think that I have not listened to you, you are wrong. I've heard your every word and your prayers, too.

If you think that I do not love you, you are wrong.
If you think that I could walk away from Our relationship, you are wrong.
If you think that My heart is pained by your pain, you are right. It is, but it is a pain that you must endure. Your pain is part of healing, growing and pruning. It is not the end result.
If you think that you have some inside track that makes you special to Me above all others, you are right. You have access to My Promises and Truth. You are like no other.

If you think that I am going to turn away from you, you are wrong. I will never leave you or forsake you. You will never leave my sight.
If you think that your lack of faith makes life harder, you are right. I know what you believe and where your mustard seed is hidden.
If you think that I will stop holding you up until you discover it, think again.

You are My love and My child. That is the best that I have for you. You are My blessing.
It does trouble Me when you begin thinking that I will abandon you. Know My heart that lives in you and silence your mind. I am here with you and you are in My heart.

There is no competition when you are with Me and I am with you.

Rejoice with Me. You have today.
My gift is now, so rejoice and be thankful!
Faint not but endure.

My Time Has Come...

I believed that being special entitled me to be heard
even when the chaos was a sound blanket to others.

The din drowned out the voices of great bards,
cantors, and even Gandhi-like prayers that God's
ears await.
"When's my turn?" I screamed out angrily.

To my right and my left, lesser people watched
sundials.
Finally, time for them stopped.
And 15 minutes later the winds called them back to
anonymity.

"When's my turn?" I screamed out indignantly.
"When will the stage be empty?"
I wondered if my time would ever arrive.
In my mind, I was taller, braver and better.
I should have stood out from the crowd.

Why couldn't they see me?
Then I noticed everyone had stepladders, stools, and
hang-gliding paraphernalia...
Even on my toes, I strained to see above the
neckline...
Till I finally, I tired and sat on the curb to look
between ankles for a clear view.

Wasn't I supposed to be elevated because of my
special skills?
Finally, I went to the forest where every tree
dwarfed me.
Sometimes I parted branches that gave a view of the
sun looking down on me.

There I learned humility, as a prelude to mediocrity.
Then I went to the meadows and lay between the
blades of grass, trying to be small.

Continued...

I looked up like a lily...a buttercup...a beetle that
clung to the stalks hiding from birds overhead.
I climbed to mountain peaks to sit atop a boulder
and behold the greatness of someone else...trying
not to fall.
I held onto ledges and kept my footing...

In my search, I have aged and weathered.
Perhaps it is time for me to sit quietly.

It is my TIME to SIT DOWN in SILENCE and know that
I am special.

New Fruit in the Garden

In that year, to celebrate your birth, I planted the
    first tree in the garden behind the house.
And two springs later when you ran across the room
    with such sure steps, I planted another.
Then and for a decade you helped me in the garden
    as you named each worm and pill bug.
The trees chronicled the passing years and spread
    branches like the arms you spread to embrace life.
Between the decades, I planted more often alone,
    sometimes leaning on the fence to catch my breath
    and seeing you off on fall evenings with friends.
Now a decade more, this small garden still boasts
    fine red apples, sweet berries and peaches that
    you have inspired.
And the trees speak of you still on evenings when
    the wind moves between leaves.
They murmur, somehow knowing that in summer or
    early fall, you will plant a first tree of your own...

The Scent of You...

The shirt that I wore last evening has the scent of your perfume in its fabric. I will not wash it but will hang it in my closet to teach other shirts how they should smell and feel.
It caresses me now and pulls me to passionate places, where my mind ought not to go during hours when a work focus is required.

And knowing full well this danger, my hands cannot help but stroke it - carrying sweetness with inadvertent movements to a sensitive nose – an olfactory and independent entity.

Now nostrils want most, to be **lips** that smile and embrace your mouth and lips. And as lips, they will only be appeased 'til your sweetness inspires them to be the **tongue** running quietly along the edge of your earlobes and the hollows of your throat.

And it in turn will cry out softly to be an **ear** that captures the sweetness of you voice saying, "Baby come here..." and will demand more words sweet and endearing...

But finally, never approaching the essence that is so much you, ALL my members will want ONLY to be the shirt that gets it sweetness by embracing you...

by Ronald Montgomery

Notes to my Readers...

The writings that follow are a departure from my normal writing and from any rules that might govern my "normal."

These are my private "scribblings" that speak to my deeply held beliefs and also include profane writings that you will not have seen in my earlier books.

Following the poems, you will find answers to questions I have received from my readers. They are taken directly from my emails. Hopefully, you will find some of your questions here, accompanied by my extended responses.

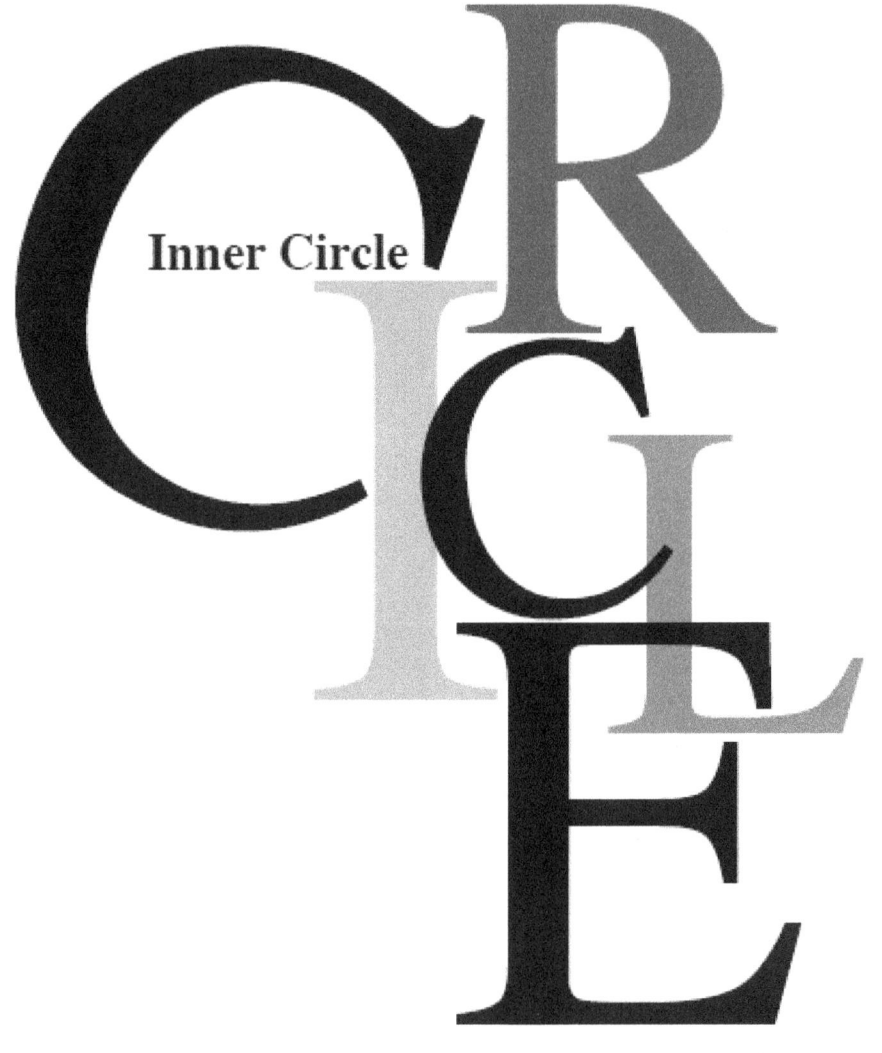

Muse

Give me a picture and I will write you a poem.
Give me your presence and I will write you a chapter.
Give me a kiss and I will write as long as your lips smile sweetly on mine.
Give me a poem and I am forever bound by a picture of "us" in my heart.

Skinny Dipping in the Moonlight

I've never been freed to go skinny dipping – covered only with a smile. How sad. Since it's not so bad and I think it's about time that I learn to swim as a matter of function – not of style.

Dipping should be easier in the buff. I hear that peace and calm help one to float, and not to sink.
Easy breathing is the release, not always to think.

I will go to St. Vincent in the dawn mist and St. John at eve's high tide, for a respite and find it, if it exists. While I cavort in the dark with new found freedom – a vacation – a Tryst

I will look behind the moon, a place for unguarded smiles that spoon.
In the dark's nite light
I'll be skinny dipping and reveling while I'm seeking,

Close your eyes.
Turn your head.

No looking!

No Peeking!

En plein air

My Love, surely you were born to the wrong century.
Claimed by another time you would have been by desires of a special
    artist, a muse - an inspiration to one.

You would have spent days on a sunny veranda, laying on the chaise -
    covered by gauze and silk to barely obscure milky parts from
    sunlight and a longing gaze.

The nearby painter would dip brushes of natural hair into oil pots and
    pigment to capture your curves - trying to focus on the scene and
    seen, as a curious breeze exposed more of your form - as if
    removing alabaster in relief for his eyes to capture...

Then, a movement and a momentary fleeting view of a perfect breast -
    recovered by nature - a falling leaf to secure the secret of innocence
    blush, while whimsical fibers hinted of "exquisite curves" hiding
    beneath.

His brush stoking a heated canvas and tarrying against distraction -
    hinted of longings to stroke your body with eyes and moist palms,
    while passionate hands moved at length across fibers receiving life
    with your image.

Now, a finally completed vision at days end - on canvas
    but you before me now - pulling my arms around
    you at night - a comforting replacement for sunlight
    and silk - my chest your starlight chaise – your body
    my canvas for stoking and stroking.

Today, we create anew...

The First Seasons... My Early Years

"These were the years when I learned about 'Strange Fruit' from Abel Meeropol and Billie Holiday.

That was the beginning – the Shoebox years, when everything was written on scraps of paper, matchbooks and napkins, and collected in a 13-D safe beneath my bed...

'Ooooh Blah Dee, Bla Dahhh' spiced my speech giving cadence to mental notes as I sat alone memorizing the waves beneath the full moon (my personal nightlight, on Carmel beach), or while riding beams and catching mist, as water collided against rocks in an attempt to follow me home from Sur...

In those days...,
Words and I became friends as they added me to their dictionary, and I added them to my family tree.
And 'Ooooh Blah Dee..., Ooooooo Bla Dahhh' set me free
To start a pilgrimage to Poet Tree.
I smile when I remember.

So now I know...
In the next seasons – the Shoebox years will be replaced by
Shoe Crate days to keyboard expression – and my poems written on texts, blogs and in clouds will be collected into the new virtual spaces of my mind...for nano mites to share in the Po Et Tree "sphere..." wherever that happens to be...

And 'Ooooh Blah Dee, Bla Dahhh' Da DoooohYA...Ooooh Blah Da' will inhabit liner notes and live in my songs – giving cadence to my dance of joy and peace on Life's Stages."

Daaa Doooyaaa Blah Daaa Daa Doooya...
Bye bye...

History for My Undoing

> The spots that mark a leopard as a leopard are its genetic
> history – inescapable.
> A pale complexion and loose naps on my head are my spots –
> a history not of my choosing.
> I am who I am, as a matter of fact, and not mine for undoing.
> The "Rape of the Virgin" is no play on words and no nuance –
> more complex than just memories.
> My reflection says muffled shouts from an obsidian sister
> went unheeded – a crime with a name.
> Buried and sometimes hidden, this is no secret to a
> community familiar with a history of shame.
> The family knows, there were no soft murmurings of "Love" –
> no care for this creation.
> The revelation – my birth was far more than disheartening –
> catastrophic – no celebrations.
> The story is the history and it lives in my skin and is not mine
> for undoing.
> The history lives on with a direct link to the past … in my
> flesh, in my reflection.
> I wonder what part of storytelling is genetic and what part is
> undocumented cultural history.
> IT refuses to die – perhaps a future vengeance on those who
> would bury the truth without a headstone.
> The real story of a nation's lies refuses to die, as long as one
> Black matriarch lives.
> She will retell the story at bedtime, by candlelight, or at the
> dining room table to all.
> My story is the history and it lives in my skin and is
> not mine for undoing.
> The words of this story are tattooed into my skin and
> woven into my naps – I know them by heart.
> I know too, that my ancestors were no willing emigrants
> and that is part of the story of lies.
> But then, I look in the mirror to see a "High Yella Brutha"
> with curly naps and green eyes.
> I wonder that I've never seen a white face in the
> generations of blackness captured in
> scrapbooks on the coffee table. Perhaps they are in
> the crack of the pages, or my image belies it.
> The pain is written in our history and it lives in my skin,
> and it is not mine for undoing.
> *Continued…*

by Ronald Montgomery

That sister, my mother didn't struggle, or raise an alarm as she became an unwilling vessel.
A mirror is a reminder that I arrived with screams on the nine-month anniversary of pain.
The reflections – the features are a visage – memories indelible that forever remain.
For a courageous woman, there is no sin, as an offering for a child spared from destruction.
Within her body's sanctuary, I was carried to safety in silence after a forced seduction.
My reflection bears witness to a legacy, not mine for undoing, but the crime has a name.
The spots that mark a leopard as a leopard are its genetic history – inescapable.
My pale complexion and loose naps on my head are my spots – a history not of my choosing.
    I am who I am, a living history that she gave a lifetime for, and now mine for undoing.
Kurotwamansa to nsuo mu a, ne ho na efo; ne ho nsensanee no de ewo ho daa.

Translation, "The leopard only gets wet when it falls into water; the water does not wash off its spots."

And So Now I Write

Your arrival
Should be herald to
Times of sweet surrender
And sultry entry into my arms
But the clocks tick silently to a rhythm not mine
And I wait for a knock that never comes
And so I write

While waiting
I have pursued sweet dreams
By tossing and turning on feathers that
Feel like rocks compared to your softness
And the moon moves silently on a path through time
And I wait restlessly for a knock that never comes
And so I write

Anticipation of your loving
Sharpens my senses to a razor's edges
To embrace and caress the softness that surrounds
And calls me to heated places and begs for
An eternity of excitement
And the darkness watches silently for approaching lights
As a prelude to the knock that never comes
And so I write

When you appear
My bedroom wants to be a shrine
That pays homage to your beauty and breasts
That calls to my lips as you fight to loose a body restrained
Waiting for a climax that will free your moans from silence
While the moon watches through parted curtains
And the clock faces away with terse reminders that
It was only my dream of a knock that never came

And so now I write

It's Just a D__K Thang...

We ALL got one...just a question of whether it's an Inny or an Outtie...
The Outtie's got some issues when the Inny's in control...
Or so this Outtie's been told
Yattta Yattta Yattta...

Cuz Inny is the Boss and ALLWAYS wins...
Butt, the Outtie noticed... There's a lot of it in here tonight, ...
You can get as many Outties as you want when UR an Inny... That can't be right...
Yattta Yattta Yattta...

The Inny always WINS!
Cuz the Inny is in control...
Is this Penis Envy, or a bill of goods I've been sold?
Yattta Yattta Yattta...

Butt, this Outtie don't want just ANY Inny, so the balls are in my court...
So you can swing your Inny to and fro...'cause I'm not that sort...
Easy on the eyes, both are in control and it's a good thang..
When a paired Outtie and Happy Inny in union SANG...
Yattta Yattta Yattta...

So the challenge goes on...to be or not be...
Control and Winning are not what captures me...
BUTT union and chemistry are what this Outtie wants to see...
Yattta Yattta Yattta...

So any way you look at it,..
Or feel it...
...Or taste it...
I guess it's just a D___K Thang!

The End

POET'S DEMENTIA

In flights of fantasy, I am a happy captive to thermals with eagle's wings. 'Though, they promise to hold me aloft forever, reality pulls me to a perch on mountain ledges. Solid rock beneath sharp talons remind me that home was first here.

It is here that I find myself in a spiritual place that knows me. There is something familiar about it, as if I have been here before.

Here there are two…who know me, not as an eagle, but as dad…
For minutes before bed and at the breakfast table en route to school…

They have never witnessed me on Carmel's beach in the still of night, watching the moon as a preamble to day, or tilting my head to hear all the sounds of waves that are really the earth's heartbeats revealed.

And I wish they had been with me to view foreign mountain passes that ushered me between gigs, or highways that were my guides to assignments and appointments to pay the bills.

I wanted to share these things before I forgot that I wrote these lines to remind me of them.

Have I written this before?

I'd sing you a song…

I'd sing you a song…
But all the words have been stolen for trite loves that pale next to you…

The lyrics are looking for lips like yours to add warmth, but they fail when YOU come into view…

The notes are melodies of songbirds compared to angels with harps…

I'd sing you a song, but only to win your heart…
To know, you'd always be mine…
Till the end of my time.

I'd sing you a love song.
For you, they are words from above.
I am singing now.

Do you hear me Love?

Bucket List...

So what's left that has gone undone as measured breathing anticipates...the final breath. What would I have done...would I still do...IF I still had time to accomplish anything...that I have not...?

I would watch the sun rise and set from my deck where I survey the waves knowing that every drop-in view is mine and that every reflected color is part of a palette created for my eyes only. It is DONE

I would sit with my child's head pressed against my chest rocking to and fro 'til restful sleep arrives... DONE

I would take my babies to the park and watch them swing and run and dance like no one was watching. DONE

I would lean back in my chair and watch you walk through the grass, with the world at your feet. DONE

I would sniff behind your ear - a flower of beauty and inhale pure fragrance scented with love. DONE

I would stand before an audience reading a poem of you that leaves no lip without a smile and no heart untouched. UNDONE but ready...

Life's PUZZLE...

Assorted...
Jumbled Pieces
Crossed words
Missed fits

New lessons today...
If memory builds into wisdom...
Would have told you sooner
Just my discovery yesterday

New jazz genre
Smooth but challenging
Dancing and learning new steps...
Sorry about the lack of parenthood
But I've never been a dad before

Sorry about the shorthanded relationship
Keyed entry..., me into you
But I've never been in love before
Never here before – in the world your leaving

Puzzled?
But I see the picture...
Now I'm finished after years of putting it all together
And now it's back in the box – all finished and going
home again.

RUNNING Too Slow

Running fleet of feet
No feat untried to escape
a specter in pursuit.

A view in the rearview of it
and me in the mirror ahead
Looking the same

What a shame "objects may be closer than
they appear"

Age has finally won.

On Rocks Below

My heart boards the flights of fancy, fantasy and
passion nightly to escape immediately to you, and I am
renewed by the dreams of being in your world...

I am transported to foreign shores and out of my
element, as I am waiting on waves only my ears will
know, crashing on rocks below
as I prepare to fall for you...

And in flight I think these thoughts as if I have any
control over where my heart will land
I find myself on shifting sands and drowning in passions
for only you.

APOLOGIES...

When I arrived, there were no tutorials
On how to be a good son.
In retrospect I apologized

In the middle, there were no instruction on manhood, nor relationships, or how to be a good husband
Looking back, I apologized

Later, there were no methods, or guidebooks
on being a good dad
With hindsight I apologized

And now, towards the end
No one can tell me what comes next, or if there's a test...
So, now with better vision, I offer no apologies

Finally, I forgive myself - apology accepted

Photos in a Shoe box

You found me and forgot me..., in just a moment in time when I looked away to some distant place and thought of neighboring worries, poignant moments of family united in a single frame, beauty uncommented and times I'd never regret.

You raised my image to the heights in that single moment, pushing others to the side, only to lose me among the hundreds of others that hid from the drips and drops of rain squeezing through holes in a damaged roof, to land squarely on my face, or on a sandy beach...

Both discolored and faded in your memories and sadly too, the paper that pictures you and me..., as you replace the lid and leave me waiting in the dark..., for your return...

I hope you will find me again.

INDELIBLE...

Memories are what they are – unchangeable pictures, even 'til eyes no longer see.
They won't offer themselves up to gesso, 'Whiteout,' or new paint.
They resist the programming of 'Photoshop' to push at pixels or remap the gamut.
Unchangeable, they'll remain even 'til seeing is no longer the eye's domain....
Memories are rust red, glacier green and chameleon hazel eyes.
They are what they are.
They are pictures of you.

Memories are what they are – unchangeable tastes, even 'til my appetite for life is sate.
No, they are not recipes for changing, or captive ingredients in my bowl.
They are not the domain of Emeril, Betty Crocker, or even my kitchen.
Unchangeable, they'll remain even 'til life's appetite for me is satisfied....
Memories are sweet, sour and earthy salt from mingled tears.
They are what they are.
They are feelings in you.

Memories are what they are – unchangeable words, even 'til meanings are no more.
Rewrites and republications of these sagas are not for Gutenberg presses.
They are not Longfellow poems, not sonnets nor Davidian psalms.
Unchangeable, they'll be even 'til words have no meaning.
Memories are stories for your recollecting and bedtime story retelling.
They are what they are.
They are about you.

Continued...

Memories are what they are – unchangeable "real,"
'til even heaven has arrived.
This is no game and "do-overs," "re-dos," or instant
replays are not allowed.
Hoyle will have no standing or sitting, nor even
reciting the rules.
Unchangeable, they'll be 'til trumpets sound and
future things are assured.

Memories are frescoes; feelings; word pictures and
our treasure chest.
They are what they are.
They are you.

And Now, they are me.

Postscript:
Written for Ryan – my Coco, on her birthday – June 21, 2011.
This day is a day of pictures, words, sensual things and
recollections. It is the day of "The Proposal."

This is a day for her collection of memories.
I pray that it is a story that she can retell often, with
a smile and sweet, salty tears. It will always be a
wonderful memory for me.

No Longer a Dream Deferred...DARE!

Like Maya, now "We will Rise and reach for a new peace!"

Being courageous sometimes means taking chances ... CHANGE! We Rise!
Being courageous sometimes means taking chances ... EXPAND!! Now, we Rise!
Being courageous sometimes means taking chances ... STAND!!! Today, we Rise!
Being courageous sometimes means taking chances ... SPEAK!!!! Tomorrow, we
    will Rise Higher!

In days of youth, and out of fear, I dared not open doors to the unknown
Later, in this latter life of mine, I have overcome anxiety only to find the distant
    meadow
A sweet expectation that I envisioned, is just beyond three padlocks and a
    deadbolt on my door
A new life perched on my threshold and pushed to be on my side as my story
    unfolds
Now I know that being courageous sometimes means taking chances and being
    bold

In my youth, the mantra of the masses was "How dare you!?"
I recoiled at reproach and doubted all I knew as true.
"Now I DO - DARE!" knowing now that what I fear MAY BE
Finding rejection's label... "Not Really... Surprise, freedom's not really free."
Now, courageous means taking chances – not invisible, but in plain view, for all to
    see

Life really is about daring to be courageous and enduring.
Chances are often the beginning of courageous and finding courage is a test of
    maturing
Our endurance from the beginning is a precursor to winning the race...
And having crossed the line, we are on pace to change the endings of history
Written in haste..., to new conclusions of peace, happiness and finally truth
Now being courageous means taking chances to arrive at victory – by elders and by
    youth

Like a poem..., the best, yet to come, may be hiding in clear view
As we look first to the *near*, and then to the *far* – discovering ideas that
May be closer than they appear, in life's mirrors just outside our doors
Even the "unlikely" IS possible if I...IF WE dare to open the doors for flight into the
    meadows

Continued...

Being courageous means no fear of flying, and now we will rise!
Now courageous, being me I shout "We the people…" as the preamble for being free…

Now I change…you stand…we speak of peace…we look to our hands to make the work complete
For our tomorrow, we will rise to the occasions – ascend to the heights courageous…
When our dreams of peace take wing and We WILL ALL RISE!!!

I DARE! You DARE!!
We DARE to dream of freedom's peace, just beginning, and to write new chapters with our lives!!!
Today We DARE! Tomorrow we DARE! Now the journey begins! Now we RISE!!!

First Seasons – Life's Improvisations

Oooooooooooh Back then….
Were the years when
'rifs and lines on paper with pen,
were much safer
when I kept them within
Jus' matchbooks and napkins,
in a 13-D coffin
thoughts, feelings and
the life I led
under my bed
and cardboard lid,
- were the secrets I hid…
Da dooya, ja DA!

Ooooh *Blah Dee,* Bla Dahhh
Spiced my thoughts
Rhymes to words I wrote
The mental notes
A Solo chorus to moonlit waves
in Early days
'Ooooh *Blah Dee,* Bla Dahhh'

Da dooya, ja DA!
Those were years
Of youthful fears
When alone
Tried to follow me home

From Sur and Carmel beaches
To Songs Life teaches…
On A pilgrimage to Poet Tree
The road to now…
The path to "Me…"
Ja Dooya Ja DA!

Words were my only friends
The rhymes next of kin
'Ooooh *Blah Dee…*
Let me be…Set me free…
To family and lovers
When all else failed
They were my family tree

Continued…

Now begins my poetry...
The Life and the Learnin'
No Turning back just emotions burnin'
Growing wisdom...Ooooooh blah Deeee
With every season...Ooooooooo blah Daaaa

Now come the days of crates
For capturing sentiments here...
And loves of late
Between lines of fiction and of fact
For me, there'll be no turning back
Ooooh yuuuuuuuu blah dee
Yuuuuuooooo Blah da...

The future beacons
New hours and seconds
For stories yet to share
And joys and dates and aire
Our heart will be sharin'
In Love we're carin'
For a world in need of new rhymes...
New times for poetry... Oooooh blah deeeeee

Shoe Crate ways
Remember shoebox days
Of keyboard expressions - improvisations
Now written as blogs *in clouds,*
Virtual spaces of my mind
for nano *mites to share at the Poet's Tree,*
Wherever that happens to be...
'Ooooh Blah Dee, Blah Dahhh' Da

DoooohYA...Ooooh Blah Da'
Inhabits my linear notes and
giving new cadence to dances of joy
Ooooooh blah deeeee...Oh Baby
And lives in my songs
 Daaa Doooyaaa Blah Daaa Daa Doooya... Ooh yeah...

Daaa Doooyaaa
And life goes on,
Blah dee Daaaa
My life's a song...

Cat's PAWs

Clearly, you have discovered that I feed on your words...
Raking my claws gently across your PJs
Words and sounds escape from you
For me to capture in my mouth –
As prisoners to ecstasy

"Oh Myyyyyyy..."
is a tasty preamble and
Hors d'oeuvres
to whet my teeth to new points

"Ummmmmmm Baby..."
delivers a first course to entrance my pallet and
Pull me closer, as my paws move
to the heartland of your jammies
With no resistance, but
slow rhythmic pushing
against the pads of my paws
"Not YEEET..." escapes
When the delta blues whine in the background and
A third course finds its way through parted lips...to linger
Wet...Fluid...motion on my tongue to tantalize...while,
"...H..m...m... m............"

Unspeakable words bind my paws
And hold my claws, as I hold tight to your thighs

"Yummmmm..."
I am moved to taste the best morsels...
A flambé – a burning desert...
Busting into sweet flames...
Brighter than stars peppering your loins
Or a full moon..., hovering close enough to touch.

And "Now... Now! ...NOWWWW!!!"
Is the aperitif that finds its way
From the tip of my tongue...
Sweet - sticky honey on the ends of my fingers...
Carried to my lips as I say "Grrrrrrr..."

And you say, "Again...?"

All That Matters

Love is what's left, when looks don't mean much anymore, but I proudly hold the hand of my **plump wrinkled beauty**.
Love is what's left when **independence is replaced by helplessness**, and the one who **feeds and freshens me** finds joy in caring for every need.

Love is what I found in the garden when
I **watched you sparing worms** while cultivating hyacinths, tulips and 'mums.
Love is what even unflattering body parts arouse when I think of the aged beauty they belonged to, and how I once held you near.

It's what's left...the best of all there ever was in my life and the best of me to you ...
It's ALL that's left worth cherishing...and what I remember even though you're gone...
Love is what's in the eyes when the last hours won't provide breath to whisper or the strength to utter.

And when I leave to join you, this page will be a legacy left to tell our children...
That Love is what's left behind.
Love is what's left to live on, and live for...
It's the best of what's left and all that really mattered, anyway.

Diamond Studs...

Sleep favors even the creative mind...
But dreams and memories are unforgiving, and treacherous friends who steal peace even from angel's rest...
A "messenger" who rises early from troubled slumber to find pierced ear-studs, searching for lobes...
The right and left remembrances of trysts a month – passing fancies, gone missing in playful moments...
Now resting on a bookshelf in search of ears missing, and nestled in repose - two diamonds in a gift box...
Awaiting another special event...
Your return

IF I am your Sea...

I will be your sea if you will be my shore
And no matter how far away I seem to go
We will touch – pushed and pulled in ebbs and flow

Silence will reign in the night save for haunted whispering
As waves of my passion move towards you...
I am impeded only by some invisible line
You have drawn
By the light of a blue moon in the sand...

I will await your sighs to pull me back into you...
As you reach out for me

If I am your sea, you are surely mine
And I will run gentle to your embrace
You will be my shore

Just Breathe...

The Promise

Your quiet sighs and night-time breathing are monuments to the love we share.
They whisper to me of all the reasons I stay.

I hold my breath to hear, in the darkness, an unguarded you that pushes against me now and again to fill the hollows of my stomach and thigh...

As you slide into my embrace – that protects you from the outside..., moans escape with nowhere to go but my waiting ears.
There..., they remain captive memories of love we've shared.

Hearing you is a clear reminder of why I've stayed so long.

Breathe for me and I will keep my promise to stay by your side.
I am listening.

Just breathe.

Mesmerized

I smell the sweetness of your skin even when you are gone.
And my nose has permanent flowery memories of you.

I am mesmerized by you and by the sensual aroma you lend to ordinary perfume to make it special. It is a wondrous event when I walk into the living room and the scent that you have left behind greets me and takes me captive – weakened and willing.

In the kitchen as I cook, sweet pastries compete for my attention
But as you pass nothing compares - ovens are forgotten as your caramel kisses fill my cups and pans to overflowing.

At my desk, as I write I am distracted away by a smell lingering between your breasts. They have brushed against the linen shirt grabbed hastily to ward off the chill of the night, but instead the fabric has ignited a flame that pulls me from my seat back to bed and into a naked embrace that fits me into you.

Now the fabric too has been mesmerized by your sweet smell.
Even at times when you are far from sight the essence of you drifts in the air, not overpowering, but as an invitation to romance and to memories of moist kisses that follow your sweetness to ecstasy.

At the end of the day, I sit in a chair that has embraced you and I remember our dance and the smell of you entrances me still.
And knowing how you have captured my heart and my mind and have put your scent in a place that I will never forget – that I want never to escape - I wait for you to appear at the bedroom door – diaphanous.

Mesmerized, I will bury my nose in the hair behind your ear and will be transported to a state of bliss as I smell your sweetness...a smell that pulls me willingly into your embrace and into you.

A Musical Labyrinth...

You are amazing and wonderful.
Your thoughts find their way to my head, into my heart and to my spirit.

You have given me reasons to write and shaped my thoughts even before my fingers begin the trail of tears and laughter to poetic lines.

I believe I hear them, even when you think silence will hide and keep them from me.

I listen to you and read letters you scribe so nimbly with those beautiful hands.

You wonder how I can capture them easily and sort them enough to rain them down in an inky response - to create a new picture, daily?

'Tis you. You are my muse and I pay attention.

I am listening... Please continue...

Fall Repose...

I will crawl between the sheets that hold you
And dream of sweet dalliances in forests of fall
Our repose colored with orange, brown and purple tree feathers
And you will disappear beneath its blanket...
To be found by my touch...your heat...our release...
The sweet perfume of your breath on my cheek
I will crawl between the sheets
For sweet repose...my hands, your lips, my nose
As one...
I will crawl between...

Good Night

Life a Reprise – Just to be Loved!

WOW...
Life passes at blazing speeds
She moves invisible to those with blinders
Who steer straight ahead, not swerving
In passing, and unceasingly
She screams out to ears that hear
That life's best ultimate message – LOVE
The word is loud, and soft, and oh so clear

Heroes have known her and echoed her songs...
Singing out refrains for all – far and near...
 "Try Love and it will heal your heart!" Mandela shouts
Martin preaches, "Give out Love and it will always
　　　return...never void!"
While Maya exhorted, "Love recognizes no barriers!"
Jesus said simply, "Love one another..., as I have loved
　　　you"
And I hunger, calling out, "I am your neighbor and your
　　　brother!
We are bound by love – one to another!"

Having fallen and risen often, the signposts passing
At the speed of life are clear – like crystal ringing, the
　　　signs...
Some hung in trees, some on walls, and other in barbed
　　　wire – bound by fear
They read, "Love Never Fails..."
For a changing world - Love changes all from a to z...
Keep love in a reservoir to make life better!
In our time, it changes you. It fixes me.

The best example for my children, that love is free...
Is Loving my neighbor who may not be like me.

Yester-Moments Now Revisited...

I have spent far too much time looking back at the days, the months and the years that have slipped away. (The sound of turning pages...)

I have spent far too much effort looking to the future and planning for what might never be, as my "now" slipped from view. (The sound of a door closing...)

Tonight, I stopped on the path with a friend and looked across the lake at a setting sun. It illuminated the underside of clouds, silhouetted trees on the distant shore, and projected reflections on the water. Click...click...

It was a spectacular moment.
I embraced it..., breathed it in..., and bit-mapped the picture into my memory (click... click...) before I turned and walked down the path.

Two steps later, I turned and looked through new foliage and remembered "yester-moment" as I focused on painting "new now" on a fresh canvas... (Swish...is the sound of a brush on rough new canvas...)

Now, is this breath... (breathing in and out...)
click...click...click...my life sequence (swish...swish...) In and out... and on to the next canvas... On to the next photograph...almost a Yester-Moment now...

SHOUT

Yesterday, PAIN was a pinprick to an ego – soon deplete of air, with nowhere to hide and no longer in disguise.

With only pleas for relief and in total despair, there was no letting go of a specter that I knew too well.

So I dwelt in prisons deep – wellsprings with no light - no moon, no sun and no stars – no exit, no "out."

The "dark night of the soul" brought my senses into keen focus on knife edges of "Grief and Pain."

Cutting deep and shallow, long and short it proclaimed itself uniquely mine – knowing only my name.

I CRIED OUT IN SHAME!

Today, I ran from "Consequences," its constant companion.

My sprint was a walk to a specter in speedy pursuit and I ran with the knowledge that loss was inevitable.

I crumbled, stumbled and fell into its embrace. I replaced it with regret and determination to change within.

With the newness of admitted failings, I found seeds of hope rooted in a fresh earth – a new creation, where my eyes opened to sweet sunrises on new horizons.

I SHOUTED AS I ROSE FROM MY KNEES!

Continued...

Now with years of tears and scars, I am grateful for experiences where I pulled back from cliff edges not daring to discover for once and for all if universal laws would prevail and be punctuated by a sudden stop.

So now, I am reassured that tripping over cracks in the sidewalk are more to my liking, and constant reminders that my pain could be worse, and that endurance brings relief, unexpected joys and better endings.

IN GRATITUDE FOR REDEMPTION I LOOK UP AND SHOUT!

Tomorrow, as a learned fool I will know not to yield. "Have faith" will become the repeated mantra of this life that brings light into dark places of anguish in longer, not shorter bursts. I will rejoice at the strength added – where the courage of weak vines is replaced with cypress trunks; and convictions that sparse overhanging branches now grown into a forest canopy will shield me from rainy downpours and let through sunbeams to guide the way home.

I WILL RAISE MY ARMS IN PRAISE AND "HALLELUJAH" TO SHOUT EVEN LOUDER!

And sometime soon – wiser, hope-filled and joyous, my convictions will carry me forward knowing that the forest gives way to glades for repose and distress gives way to relief on cool spring days and nights that are moonlit and starry.

Moreover, I will rejoice knowing that grace and mercy will follow me all the days of my life and pain will be replaced with jubilation, if I endure.

FOR A LIFE REDEEMED, I SHOUT SELAH AND HALLELUJAH!

Waiting on You Reprise

Throughout the day, I would cast furtive glances at my email hoping some writer's name would be familiar...
No not today..., and so searching eyes very much resembled the skies with clouds obscuring the sun for one...
And now at day's closing I find there are scripts posing as email and haiku that come from you and I am grateful and eager...
That one meager line on a long list of emails could bring a smile as would summon the light of a near star!!!
Now a door ajar leaks bright into the night outside causing flowers to wake as if springtime has arrived early and darkness never...
Away with shadows and gloom, as I read your words...and now I smile

Reflection on "Waiting."

Anyone who has served in the military and been stationed away from home, knows the expectations associated with getting mail from loved ones.

In my years before personal computers, there were paper letters with red lip-prints for safeguarded contents, under protection with first class stamps, delivered at "Mail Call."

On later tours, letters were emails. The experience is the same – ELATION. Sometimes, that email was the brightest spot in a day of fear, sadness and resignation.

Warriors paid the high price extracted for service in hostile places and being separated from home. We hoped for email that would bring love from home on torrid days. These moments of respite were often the fuel we needed to see us through exhaustion and nightmares about things that went BOOM in the night.

Fall Repose Reprise of Tree Feathers

I will crawl between the autumn sheets to hold you
And dream a sweet dalliance in forests hues
Our repose covered with orange and purple tree feathers
A respite from work and worries and things that matter
As you I plunge to depths – into earth and moss
Beneath a blanket to be found by my touch…
your heat…our release…a leafy crunch
The sweet perfume of your breath on my cheek
I will crawl through airy spaces…nature's sheet
On a Fall lawn, we will rest and dream together
in leaves raked for our afternoon's sweet repose
…my hands, your lips, your hair, my nose
What a wonderful day to begin resting till Spring's rebirth

And Now I Sleep

Having done all that was required of me…
And exhausted my resources and strength
I lay down for quiet repose
Certain that no one knows that I have been haunting the
halls and rooms where life's work and love reside
But now I have done all that I can do
And sleep calls me gently away to rest
I've done my best and none will know 'til dawn
That now I sleep

ALZHEIMER

I fear the possibility and specter of lost awareness,
and lost control...
This moment is all I have...
This moment is all I have...
I fear the possibility and specter of lost awareness,
and control...
Have I told you what I fear...?

Fallen Angel

I was always a messenger...
Long before you beheld me...
I plummeted to earth...
My feathers in the grass at my feet, ...
And my wings – now invisible...
Continued to embrace and shield you

Do you not see what you have done to me...?
I was always an angel...for you
I fell to the meadow...
beside you..., smitten

Long before you beheld me...
I had already fallen...
for you...

Salvation for the Next Generation

"Let the church say AMEN!"

Grandma prayed and Mama prayed
While I played in the clubs and danced my life away
The church sang their songs and service went long
'Til the pastor's benediction end and "the congregation said AMEN!"
I did my thing, with no regard for time or consequence – throwing caution to the wind
I enjoyed life and ran with my friends 'til the moon said goodbye to the morning skies
Not really knowing at the beginning, any wisdom for living, I stayed in the streets
And in my naiveté, I was the son that made my mother moan and weep
Who was she praying for anyway, when the house couldn't sleep?

Then the church prayed
While mama rocked back and forth to a chorus of "Amazing Grace"
And the pastor's talk droned on and on while I searched for a way out
Making youthful plans for tonight's diversion – planning my sins while the church sang amen...
I smiled and mocked ...moving on down the street
Not really knowing the consequences or the wisdom verses for living
I tempted fate and never playing straight, not realizing that lessons in life aren't free
Thinking my youth was forever – doing whatever I chose – it was all about me
Concerned only for self, I had my way paid not mind to my parents weeping
Who were they praying for anyway, when they thought that I was sleeping?

And Madea prayed "Save my baby – he just doesn't know..."
While Mama sang in the choir, a chorus for new beginnings and everlasting
Life's not just doing his thing – bring him home, so I'm praying and fasting
While the church intoned "Aaaaaaaamen..." with countless intercessions, I stayed

Outside the door and the body, I made a name for myself –keeping all my cred...
Not really knowing the consequence of street wisdom vs wise living
Some nights I ran and dodged and arrived home almost dead
And in my ignorance, I lay down to regain my strength – in the other room, mama wept.
Who was she praying for anyway? Calling out my name...! Humph, so I slept?
Half a decade since and now I hear my sweet wife pray
While mama, swayin' and singin' to a baby that looks just like me
While the choir sings and the deacon prays, he coo's "gam-ma... Amen"

Continued...

While I work overtimes and third shifts...and anytime jobs
To buy groceries, light the house, make ends meet and just to pay the rent
Now with my head on a swivel, I pay attention on walks to work, the store and my door as
Danger Prowls hungry on our streets - waiting to steal and kill, and make parents weep
Now, praying never ceasing... "If I should die before I wake...I pray the Lord my soul to keep..."

Today, I pray "Save my son, my only one..."
My wife prays while Mama intercedes and weeps
And from the pulpit I preach with new wisdom – my spirit no longer asleep
I pray to keep all our families free and safe from harm
That the Spirit of our God protect us and lead us NOW
Let the church say, AMEN!

1600 Penn 2016

That's too bad, but it's not here and it's not me...
It will be someone else's problem until the birds come home to roost... My isn't that nice straw.
Chirp chirp...

AND THEN I Smiled...

My creative child emerged on a daily romp to the mall...
As I listened to the music and knew the muse within...
I smiled once...and then twice...and then once again...
How wonderful a smile felt when it knew it was supposed
to be about playing across my face...and kneading lips
to create laugh lines around my mouth and eyes
to express happy that coursed within...
through a heart that knows the true meaning of Joy
Laughing out loud to a chorus of "Man, am I blessed..."
I gave the world clues and then another, and yet another...
Contagious, it spread like the wind...as one person smiled
To another...and another, and then once again...
Creative children emerged on daily romps in the world...

Intentional Living

Now, Now, a "Now" and another NOW
A string of pearls that tell of being in joy, of hope, of pain, grace and mercy
Some shining brightly; some dulled by troubled waters; some newly created and irregular
However, all accepted with open eyes and understanding that not all things beautiful begin that way.
In the beginning of my "365 storytelling", I put on my "life-suit" – blanketed and covered in experiences enough for "wrapped-up" and "bowed-on" a package of "Me" with all the intentions of being genuine.
Living with the little I knew, I passed off "streetwise" as wisdom and survived until understanding finally arrived.
Then living honestly applied all the necessary features to a ruddy countenance and brushed on the blush of naïve.
Later the tarnish of romances and love-less passions darkened my browns, purples and pinks to bruises of hard knocks.
The mist of sensitivity-pain-filled-heartbreaking-crushing rejection-seasoned-tears flowed from heart-connected-faucets, until the hurt in my chest spread through a trembling frame and reached into my mind to name experiences of shame.
Books in my "life-library" mimicked Dante, (James) Baldwin, Steinbeck and (Richard) Wright dramas,
I called them reminders of my reality and labeled them programming tools to hardwire me to "Real" and "Authentic."
Along the crest of my ears were rings and piercings – markings visible and NOT – medals I sported after receiving, passing on and filtering "life scripts" through willing ears to become an apt discerner – staying in contact and "being Present."
Conversations exited parted lips, making me a member of the cast and purveyor of oral traditions.

Continued...

by Ronald Montgomery

But most of all, I came to realize what really saturated
    my actions and words – the real me.
An actor, my lips were crimson for the harlot I became in
    trading truth for moments of success and prosperity.
Hands were rough from holding tight to life getting by -
    leaving smoldering flesh from the friction.
Gradually, I wiped away the affectations to embrace the
    effectuations of a world reaching out to touch me.
I connected the plugs to the power sources and
    energized my living for achieving beyond meager –
    for giving and forgiving beyond my norm to grow to
    a new normal of truly happy and connected.
Rough skin softened to supple for embracing and
    touching, and finally for holding onto other's hands
    reaching out.
I now look squarely into the reflection of my past living
    and release intentions to influence future twists and
    events of love, of community, and of family, now
    that I am in the company of a Spirit I know as "Dad."
As a backdrop of days and years forgone, I now write
    pages in my daily diary entitled
"Today on a Path to Intentional Living."

The Next Seasons – Looking Ahead

On my Tomorrows
My time will be spent connected to spirit-filled endeavors, exploring dreams and visions that go beyond worldly understanding. I will tap into the energy that fuels my words and connects your experiences to mine.

"For the next seasons – the Shoebox will be replaced by a **Shoe Crate** – and everything written on texts, blogs and in clouds will be collected in the new virtual spaces of my mind...

And Da DoooohYA...Ooooh Blah Dee Bla Dahhh will spice my speech and songs, giving cadence to my dance of joy and peace on Life's Stage.

And I will sit beside my queen on our deck contemplating the ocean beneath the moon – our personal nightlight – above Carmel's beach."

A Gift

My favorite time of day for writing is at night while everyone in my part of the world is sleeping soundly.
Or at sunrise when everything is realizing that life abounds anew.
In the night, I am at peace... In the morning I am revived and stimulated.

I change the world while the world sleeps. They never realize that anything is different when they wake.

Continued...

One line…and one night at a time, I add color and
    contours, and sculpt away jagged rock to reveal
    a shoulder…, a hand…, a foot…, parted lips…

At some point, I uncover and color stone to stand
    among Art Hill's "old work" with no fanfare.
Only I am aware, that there is now something new,
    and it owes its existence to quiet work beneath
    the stars, before the sound of birds sing in the
    new day.

The world will never know that I have left a present
    for them, until I announce it at some reading.

I will call it a gift and they will call it poetry.

The Journey is Not Over

MY PAIN INFORMS TOMORROW of my imminent arrival and reminds me that I am alive – that yesterday was far from perfect…and that the Journey is not over till hope prevails to victory's ends… But until then, I will march on, adding friends, family and community to a parade through barren landscapes to flowery fields of grass and restful completion in final repose…who knows, maybe tomorrow's beginning will signal an end to sad faces and tear traces with salt trails…on the faces of rainy-day sisters and brothers…
Until then the journey is not over

Letting Go

It is the best act of spiritual healing – kindness –
 opening the door again to love.
With your hands on my chest I ask, "Where are the
 burdens? Where are the weights?"
What matters the conversations – how or when words
 were spoken that should never have been?
Why were two souls moved to corners – unreconciled
 to life, and of love deprived?
How could things of no value turn plains into mountains
 - creating peaks bounding a grand canyon?
Was the distance just to be out of sight – hearts
 burdened with the need to be right?
When life is done, I will have a last wish before
 breathing deep and closing my eyes to sleep.
I will thank you for the gift you have waited so long for
 me to receive - forgiveness.
It will be what I take and give in return – thankful for
 more than I have earned.
The best act of kindness I welcome and value – your
 grace, mercy and love.
My bags will be empty and no longer anchored to guilt, I
 will be light enough to fly.
All will be done when I am free to go, soaring off to the
 heavens with mean feelings below.
Alas, I am forgiven! Thank you for letting go.

Salty Tears

Tears are a needed drink to a wild rose in a field of lilies.
A torrential downpour to my soul gratefully discovering the end of drought.
Life, giving life to something new - to wash away things I have come to know.
Cooling rains come to extinguish smoldering embers and prevent them from reigniting.
Confirmation to those held close that we share far too much pain in anger with those we love.
A test of authentic for past regrets, and an eyewash for perfectly crafted and poignant memories.
A trail with salty tracks that paves a way through fleshy deserts for renewal, leaving a fresh path to joy.
A plea "Forgive me...?" now in the company of an unburdened heart.

Questions from my readers...

Answers to Your Questions - Introduction

In the pages that follow, I answer questions frequently asked by my readers.

I have not answered every question. By my nature I am quite a private person. However, as I write poetry I have alluded to virtually every aspect of my life. That being said, I tried to respond to the most persistent questions.

If you have a question that has not been answered here, I will entertain it for a response in a next publication, or directly at my email.

I can be reached via email at spirit2spirit.poetry@yahoo.com. Please indicate "Reader Question" in the subject line. I will always respond directly to you, even if only to say that I have received your email. If time permits and my need for privacy is not compromised, I will answer the question immediately.

Thank you for your support, and for your positive intentions expressed in your emails and feedback.

Question: When did you begin writing? Why did you begin writing? Why do you continue writing?

Answer: In 1974, I began to write. I was in the U.S. Army, studying German at the Defense Language Institute, in Monterey, California. Strangely enough, the writing I did was not for me, but was for peers who knew that I could turn a poetic phrase. I wrote love letters and poems for friends for their loves.

I have continued writing. The scraps of paper, and matchbook covers on which I jotted ideas, found a home in a shoebox beneath my bed.

Since I began, I've written thousands of pages. I had no particular reason for saving all the bits and pieces of poems. I did keep them, and I am glad that the urge to purge and discard were not compelling enough to throw them away.

Some of these pages found their way into my books of poetry. Although, I never intended to make them public. Other ideas languish on napkins and scraps of paper in the same shoebox. They are awaiting completion. Still others will remain private journal entries that my children may one day find and read. They are not hidden, just not published.

The lessons and poems in this anthology are not sequential. Many of these were written during my radical years when I wanted to be like Langston Hughes, Nikki Giovanni, or Huey P. Newton.

This penchant is evident in poems like "J. B. Simple (ly) Enlightened" and "a letter to God." I was angry, sad and frustrated during these years. My writings embraced these emotions and spilled out onto the pages while my daily life mirrored my struggle to understand why I felt so much anger, fear and uncertainty.

Other poems were written in the process of discovering the meaning of intimacy and love. Still, more poems were written as I learned to differentiate between these concepts during the seasons of my life. Sometimes the changes and lessons were obvious in my writing. At other times, they are subtle and disguised.

My writing was never intended to be a vehicle for sharing my feelings. My poems were part of a disjointed journal that documented my life-lessons and how I incorporated them.

Lesson one — Living life fully does take skills. It is not like falling off a rock... That is especially true, if I am trying not to repeat Humpty Dumpty's fatal mistake.

Generally speaking, this anthology and all my books chronicle the basic course of my journey with side-trips to:

Finding Meaning
Finding Myself
Finding Love
Finding the Words to express my emotions...

I thank God for allowing me to live through the turbulent times it has taken to write these poems. It is only by His grace, influenced in large measure I am sure by the vast number of prayers from my mother, that I am here to share these lines with you the reader. In retrospect, I know that prayer works. I am the living proof.

Question: Has writing changed you?

Answer: Absolutely and permanently. No part of my being has been left untouched. Although my essence has not changed radically, even it has grown to keep pace with my monumental metamorphosis of the holistic "Me."

Question:" Do you find writing emotionally draining?"

Answer: Yes and no. It is draining and invigorating at the same time.

Frequently when I write, I draw from all the things that are in my house. That is "my metaphorical house" that I bring to the keyboard.

As my fingers hit the keys, I draw from the experiences which reside like furniture and ghosts in its rooms.

Some memories, I have stored in the basement and avoid, because it's dark and maybe damp down there. These seldom find their way directly into my poems but do influence and provide a nuanced view of some lines. This is not a peaceful place. But they are not totally ignored. Some of my poems to address issues that were seldom discussed in earlier years. One of these is suicide. Most everyone I know has dealt with these thoughts at some point. This even includes me.

Some material comes from the attic. "WOW, I haven't seen that in a long time." These are the pleasant memories and things that are not intimidating or challenging. They are just dusty, but still serviceable.

Other experiences come with fresh perspective to the front door. I sometimes usher them inside and provide hospitable places in the living room, or at the kitchen table.

Some events come in through the windows when I am trying to ventilate and get a fresh view. Still others come into the sunroom riding on rays, or moonbeams at night. They fall upon an unsuspecting me and bring revival and new insights. They rouse me and move me sometimes reluctantly to the keyboard in my library.

And there are times when I need to be fed and hunger is illusive. I graze aimlessly in the refrigerator sampling until just the right morsel satisfies me.

Then of course, some inspiration comes from my boudoir where all the above manifest again... She arrives while I toss and turn with purpose – sweating as I, the cunningly illusive prey, now become the predator.

Or she beckons, as I lie on some resilient grass covered slope or cool meadow dreaming, and waiting for deeper repose or her nubile company...

Then there are all the passions and visions of hopes, and daytime dreams that come alive.

Imagine... All of this happens every time I sit down to write. It is happening now, even as I pen this response.

The ONLY time that I can lock away these influences is when I work at my traditional job. Here, my pragmatic mind intervenes and intercepts, and builds walls without doors or windows, to keep me in check.

So, between the hours of 2 and 4 AM, or 5 as it was this morning, my mind is very busy...and FREE.

Sometimes the words overload my fingers. The memories flood over me as my mind's eyes see replays of the past and recollect conversations verbatim.

At times, the 'Backspace' key wins out. Then many of the sentences return to blank places on the page and words are chased back into hiding.

And sometimes the tears win out, when the delete key is overruled for the healing expression and catharsis.

When my writing time ends, I am exhausted and am ready for sleep. I do a "Save." I stand, leaving my office chair spinning slowly and turn off the light.

I walk through the darkness, back to the bedroom, often forgetting to turn off the computer, or counting on the 'screensaver' to save the phosphors from 'screen-burn.'

Sometimes I wonder what happens when I am out of sight. I suspect that the light inside the monitor somehow knows that there is limited time, now that I have gone, to let words escape into the darkened room and out into the world.

When I return and press any key, the words have returned in search of some completion that only I can provide.

Thank you, for asking the question.

Question: Why do you write NOW?

Answer: FREEDOM, LIBERATION and WINGS...

I've talked to my motorcycle riding friends. They describe the feeling associated with motorcycle riding as "a sense of freedom." The friends who sky dive talk about experiencing "...the ultimate thrill of flying like a bird. It is an extreme adrenaline rush of exiting a perfectly good airplane to land 2 or 3 miles down!" Imagine jumping out at about 25 miles above the earth like Felix Baumgartner. That's the feeling I get when I write.

The pleasure is sustained and repeatable as long as my parachute opens prior to landing. So far, my chute has never failed me. I continue to dive into a morass of issues as I explore every crevice of my humanity. So far, the exploration has not done harm and has yielded a wealth of insight and I dare say "wisdom."

Let me answer the question in a slightly different way. The freedom is what happens to me when I discover something new about myself. It is when I find a new part of myself as a result of the effort. I gain insight into who I really am. I discover some new insight into why I have done something in my life.

So here is a recent example. I shared this insight with a friend of mine during a recent walk.

As I answer questions from my readers, I have discovered that at some point in the past, I have unwittingly developed a way of sharing the experiences of virtually everyone that I meet.

On the walk, my friend described the experience of waterskiing in great detail... Vicariously, I embraced every word in the description. I found myself holding onto the rope behind the boat and slicing through the water. At one point I crossed the wake of the boat and almost lost control. I recovered in time and slipped back into the channel behind the boat.

Now how is that possible? My friends laugh since they know that I have a fear of being in the water if my feet are not solidly planted on the surface below.

So now you know. I get to live vicariously through my ability to be empathetic. Sometimes, that can be enough. And so I write.

Question: Do you have any regrets?

Answer: Yes. One of my biggest regrets is that I did not leave a pad of paper by the bed the night when I dreamt the best poem ever. As I slept, I remember vowing not to forget. Upon waking I couldn't remember any of it. But I can still feel the lingering traces. I am tantalized by how good the lines were, but I can't remember a single word.

Other regrets, I keep to myself, until I write them in my poems. They are there if you read the poems.

Question: Was there ever a time that you doubted yourself and your writing ability?

Answer: Yes, every time I read a piece of what I consider to be my best work. LOL. I am sure Da Vinci felt the same when he described a machine that could fly. Smiles.

In truth, I always doubt the goodness of my writing, and think sometimes that I am killing trees needlessly. At other times, I feel the inspiration and it spills out onto the paper. I am impressed for a moment. Then I reread it days later and wonder if I was in my right mind, or wonder even "Who wrote this? It's far better than anything I have written."

There are a range of responses that I experience.
The confirmation of any goodness is when I am approached by a reader who begins to cry when recounting one of my poems because it touched a buried emotion. That is the feedback that I need to continue working on my poems. And so I write.

Question: Have you ever written a poem and immediately deem it "perfect" and never edit or re-write it? If so, reveal one...

Answer: Yes. This has happened several times that I can remember. However, they were always parts of dreams, the details of which I forgot as soon as I woke. See the answer on regrets. Smiles.

The ones that remain untouched after the first writing are normally shorter poems that I scrutinize and cannot find a flaw with the logic. These are frequently the ones that come from some inspired moment for which I have idea of the origin of the concept. Read "Rainy Day Sister."

Question: Do you keep everything you write, even if you don't like it?

Answer: Yes. Every scrap of paper is like a seed. Imagine having a bag full of flower seeds. Not every seed will grow. Some are dormant. Some are dead. But you can never tell by looking at them, which is which. They will need to be cast to the ground, watered and watched. The ones that grow will need tending.

I have written pieces that refuse to be more than random black dots scattered on white cellulose – dead seeds. Others grow in size and hue and create word pictures – lush meadows.

I always hope for the best. But, like comparing myself to Da Vinci, some things just don't translate into brilliance, beauty or life.

Question: Your poetry "stirs up" images that could sometimes be considered erotic for your readers. Have you ever been approached by readers who want to draw you in personally?

Answer: Really? As a rule, I avoid conversations about how my readers evaluate my writing at an emotional or sensual level when talking one-on-one. I know the effect I am trying to achieve with each poem. Although, I do encourage my readers to write me emails with feedback.

Most often, my focus is on describing the events or ideas from my vantage point, and not relating someone else's feelings, unless the poem is about how I believe someone else feels or shares a story that has made an impression on me.

Every reader brings their own perspective to my poems. Sometimes they are different and sometimes they are similar to mine. Oh well...

As selfish as it may seem, sometimes, I do not want to be influenced by how others perceive my writing. I want to be unaffected and unencumbered. For the most part, I succeed.

Additionally, I never want to cross what I believe is an ethical line. My writing was never meant to open doors to relationships – at least not as romantic conversation starters.

Question: Have members of your family read your books? Have they made comments about your works?

Answer: That is an interesting question. The answer is a source of some sadness.

I began writing my books to provide reference points for my children. I wanted to tell them more about the father that worked far too many hours and spent far too much time being concerned about material things, tuition and utility bills.

My writing is not a fix for what I can never change. It is instead a salve for wounds that will remain for a lifetime.

I do believe that some wounds heal. However, for someone with a vivid memory, each time I remember bad decisions..., choosing material over experiences, I still wince in pain. Forgiving myself is a high mountain to climb. For some things, I sit quietly on the mountain top. For others, I sit at the mouth of a cave contemplating the next part of the climb to the top. With some luck and support, it may happen that I can see the mountain range completely before leaving this place.

I talk a lot about this journey in my poems. I believe my writing has succeeded at sharing motives for my actions and my best intentions, regardless of the unintended consequences. Hopefully, my wise children will understand and forgive a father who has always been in love with them, and not just belatedly.

I digress. My children and family are impressed that I have written so much and even recorded CDs of poetry. However, they see me as immanently accessible and a permanent fixture. And as with most permanent fixtures, they become part of everyday living and may not stand out from the background.

I am a poet and virtually all conversation is tinged with some poetic line or philosophy.

I sometimes laugh when I suggest that everyone may find time to 'read me' when I am departed.

For me, that means when I retire to the coast and not from planet earth. I hope. Smiles.

Question: What other poets or writers do you admire and/or read?

Answer: The poets that I admire and read on occasion are Nikki Giovanni, Maya Angelou, Langston Hughes, Eugene Redmond, and Gregory Pardlo.

The style of these writers resonates with me. I am not drawn to write like them, but definitely understand that they are more than mere poets. They are storytellers.

My style of writing is more like theirs than any of the other traditional or contemporary writers.

I have been critiqued by some readers and peers who insist that as a writer, I should read the greats. Perhaps it would do me some good. This could be true.

However, my perspective for now is that I am probably more of a 'primitive.' I do not insist on changing, influencing, or impacting anyone else. I, likewise, do not aspire to write like, emulate, or replicate the style, or the work of anyone else. Additionally, when I write, I am not bound by volumes of rules or traditions. That being said, I try never to end a sentence with a preposition. Smiles...

And honestly, I am too busy trying to find time to do my own writing – expressing the complexities of my life and attending to the events that flood over me from NPR (National Public Radio), to have time to read the "greats."

Perhaps I will when I retire to the ocean and have stopped struggling to develop my own style. Nikki suggests that I never stop practicing my craft. Maybe, one day I will be among the greats to my children, and I will have read and learned more from other "Great Poets/Bards."

Question: Some of your poetry is heavy. Is it sobering or disturbing when you read it, too?

Answer: "Sobering" and "Disturbing" ... These words are sobering and disturbing when I think of them in connection to my writing.

I certainly hope that my writing inspires both of these.

I find life to be frequently joyful, sometimes sobering, oft times disturbing, and gratefully energizing and peaceful at the same time.

I am not in denial about what is the "nature of the beast." Rocks make for great foundations and they hurt when they fall from high places to smack one in the forehead. Ouch... But they have no ill intentions.

I build each line of my poetry with this life formula. I find my poetry to be much like the life that crafted me and recognizing this I am reaffirmed.

I hope that my poetry is reaffirming to my children and to my readers. I hope that it is sobering enough to move them to away from things that would harm them and disturbing enough to move them towards goals that make this a better and more loving world.

Question: What is your favorite time of day to write?

Answer: My favorite time of day for writing is at night while everyone in my part of the world is sleeping soundly. Or at sunrise when everything is realizing that life abounds anew.

In the night, I am at peace... In the morning I am revived and stimulated.

I change the world while the world sleeps. They never realize that anything is different when they wake. One line...and one night at a time, I add color and contours, and sculpt away jagged rock to reveal a shoulder..., a hand..., a foot..., parted lips...

At some point, I uncover and color stone to stand among Art Hill's work with no fanfare. But I am aware...that there is now something new, and it owes its existence to my quiet work beneath the stars...or my stimulations at the sound of birds singing in the new day.

The world will never know that I have left a present for them, until I announce it at some reading.

I will call it a gift and they will call it poetry.

Question: Do you have a significant other? If you don't, why not?

Answer: The answer is yes. Since I am very private on the face of things, I will direct you to my poems to know more about the "One."

I have discovered that I am not "easy..." I am lovable but loving me is not an easy thing. At best, I have just recently learned to love me unconditionally. Consider "recently" in terms of a decade or so.

by Ronald Montgomery

Question: Do you think that your works contribute to the arts of expression for people of color?

Answer: I don't know. I am very aware of my experiences, my culture, my identity and my history.

Far from being just aware, I am hyperaware of my humanity. My goal is to forget the awareness of my color..., my sexuality..., my baldness..., my emotions..., and remember the most important thing of all. I am part of something larger and far more important than me.

My desire and intention for the rainbow coalition that I call humanity, is that we focus more on fixing injustice, inequality and our inability to get beyond "stupidity and ignorance."

These are my focal points even when I point to things like the color of my skin, or my naps. It's not about the feature. It is about the fact that "strange fruit" should make us all want to cry and fix our world.

What I do with my words is not an art. It is just one brother talking to another sister or brother and making a point that spears "wrong" squarely in the heart.

We will fix this, or it will be our demise.

Question: If you were to set forth a goal for your writing or exposure as an artist due to your works, what would that be?

Answer: My goal is JUST ONE MORE MEANINGFUL poem that steps away from the mundane and trite.

Just ONE MORE... that moves humanity from night to light...

Just ONE MORE that makes a sad heart sing...

Just ONE MORE... Just ONE MORE...

Do you feel me...?

Question: Some of your words are so beautifully constructed and strung together. Is there a common source to your inspiration? How do you determine what you will write about?

Answer: I have no idea where most of the insights or words will originate... They just happen when I least expect it.

Okay, I do know one source, but no one seems to want to hear it or accept it.

Here's the truth. My inspiration always comes from the Holy Spirit. See, I told you. Call IT what you want... The energy and inspiration are waiting. I am just a messenger and a miner. I look for the vein and sometimes I hit pay dirt.
This is what happens. I receive an inspiration. I write it down and then I wait for it to develop. Words are written without much regard for content, or style. I return to it later and polish it repeatedly. When it tells me that it is finished, I stop polishing.

Frequently, I read my writing after leaving it for weeks or months. I am frequently amazed and wonder how I could have written this. The words almost seem foreign to me. It must be the messenger's work...

Question: Do you have a method of bringing experiences back so you can re-examine them and write about them? If so, please share...

Answer: Although I try to live all of my life in the moment, the past is never really absent but standing in the other room out of sight and waiting for my return.

As long as I don't forget how to get to the door and unlock it, I can relive the events. There are many rooms in my house.

Forgetting is a gift sometimes, I think. However, it is not a gift that I have received. I believe my dyslexia adds to this. The writing and reading are a challenge, but the remembering is fairly easy to me.

While in grad school, I discovered that I have a form of dyslexia. I always knew that my retention was never from written words. I remember and retain dialogs – things I hear. This has frequently been a source of annoyance when I repeat movie or play dialog verbatim after once hearing it.

So, here's the thing. When I walk through the door to the past, it is as fresh as if it is now. Sometimes it tries to crowd out the "now." So, in an effort to forget, I give it a new room, a little further down the hall.

When it lives in my writing, I can finally put it on a shelf. It is out of sight, but I know where to find it.

Question: If, you were to write your own epitaph – when your journeys are done, what would you want it to say?

Answer: It would recount my last conversation with God.

It would say… "Thank you, Father. You've made all my dreams come true and have given me a reason for being here. **WOW! Cool Beans! What's next?**

I can hardly wait. Oh, I don't have to, now! -)"

Question: Are you a "spiritual person?"

Answer: Yes, at least by my standards.

I am a bit of an odd duck and I thank God. I seldom tell others my deeply held beliefs. This is primarily because I don't need company as confirmation of what I believe. And I definitely don't want anyone following me, thinking I have some special insight. I too, am a traveler on this road. It may be a road that crosses yours, or that runs in parallel. I have seen others in my travel, but often they were in the distance, in front of me, behind me or sometimes beside me.

For my entire life, when I have been asked who I am and why am I here, I have answered "I am a messenger." And, if you are able to translate that into Aramaic, you will know who I really am.

That was and is my response made with no elevated thoughts of my importance or worth.

I'm just the guy who channels what I get from God and delivers whatever message I am given. No, not every poem is a message. Smiles. Sometimes, I am playing with words, and entertaining myself and my readers.

And no, I am not a "New Age" Christian. I am just a guy who has a relationship with God and finds great joy and peace in it.

As humans, we seem to be so fixated on what we think we understand. I am expectant and anticipating the joy of discovering things beyond my comprehension, or wildest expectations, when I go to the next stage of my being. My frequent response to questions about the Spirit is "Who knows?" I don't have the answers for anyone besides myself, and I am still searching.

There are so many things at play in our lives and the best evidence we have of what is beyond our sight, are the revelations of our intuition. Knowledge is far less important than the intellectuals among us think.

From what I know, "We should look to the creations around us, and remember our limitations lest we think too highly of ourselves... There are so many clues that point to a higher power.

In my opinion, we should operate less based on our intellect. It frequently leads us astray."

This life is just the beginning, and that belief is sobering.
This is not the end. This is not my end.

Question: Is there a central theme to your writing that develop in your books?

Answer: The common thread for many of my poems is loving life, even when it seems that life is not reciprocating.

In my opinion, life is about the pursuit of happiness, being connected and completion. These efforts always couple with "finding and expressing meaning, truth and love" to arrive at joy and peace. When we consciously or unconsciously believe that this is done, we have run the race and arrived at the finish line.

For me, and hopefully for the many who read these lines, the efforts of finding and expressing "True Love" is on-going. Finding that love is not the end, but just the beginning of something even more wonderful.

The boundaries for love continue to move out, expanding its scope exponentially. For non-physicists like me, that's "bunches!" For the scientists, it means reaching for the edges of the expanding universe.

How simple, right?

Question: Is there any advice that you would give an aspiring writer?

Answer: I have learned two lessons that I view as critical. The first is "Be diligent." The second is, capture every idea as quickly as possible.

By diligence, I mean that developing writing skills is often a function of writing every day for some specified time. The amount of time comfortably writing, varies from person to person. The length of time appears to increase as a function of the length of time that this regimen is practiced. I began writing for 20 minutes each time I sat down to create. I now spend hours that seem like minutes.

Identify the best time for you. The best time of day differs from person to person. I write at my most creative time – between midnight and five in the morning. I am not recommending that you sacrifice sleep. I am suggesting that when you find the most productive time for you, the exercise is more pleasant, and developing writing endurance is less of a chore.

The love of writing expands the window from minutes to hours. It is a time machine. Time gets away from you and before you know it, hours will have passed.

The second recommendation is to "capture everything." Write it down. It does not matter that it is not perfect. It does not matter that it is not complete. When it is written, it will develop a life of its own. It will grow and will be perfected over time.

As I told a fellow writer…, "If you don't write the idea down, it will become the property of another." The ideas seem to have a way of being born either in my mind or in the mind of someone else.

They will not be silenced or ignored. They are like seeds looking for fertile moist ground to germinate and express themselves as a flower, a leaf…, a tree, a grain, or a piece of fruit.

When Heart's Surrender

She is the last and greatest love of a wonderful life.
At field's edge, she stands among lilies, daisies and tall grass.
Having crossed rivers and mountains to stand beside her, I clear the
    earth around my love's stem.
Sitting with crossed legs, we are together to watch the setting suns as
    preludes to moonlit nights.
Knowing our end time is nigh; I savor her bouquet and memorize her
    lines, knowing
That when her last petal falls to earth, my love for flowers will end and
    I will say adieu.
I will have painted her image in my heart to keep until it is my time,
    too

SO, what did I learn...?

The "One Thing and the Real Secret" of my life is that there is NOTHING more important than love. When all is said and done, it is the love that is the single thread that ties everything together. It is the essence of authentic relationships, and it will be the essence of who we are that is left behind when we depart this place.

All the education... All the money... All of these in combination with all the power mean nothing if this critical element goes missing from our daily encounters with others.

I have learned this, and I hope you have also.
Be BLESSED and know that as you read this line, I am sending you love and all the best intentions.

Postscript

I would like to thank you for taking the time to read the poetry I've shared here. This book is also available as an eBook for virtually all personal reading devices.

I value the feedback from all of my readers and encourage you to drop me a line, either to make comments, or to ask a questions.

My email, as noted earlier is Spirit2spirit.Poetry@Yahoo.Com. Please put the name of the book in the subject line to get my attention.

I offer my best intentions for you and the most sincere blessings from my heart to yours.

Thank You
Ron

CPSIA information can be obtained
at www.ICGtesting.com
Printed in the USA
BVHW010432201022
649857BV00005B/71